ACOUSTIC BLUES GUITAR STYLES

ACOUSTIC BLUES GUITAR STYLES

LARRY SANDBERG

Routledge
Taylor & Francis Group
New York   London

Routledge is an imprint of the
Taylor & Francis Group, an informa business

Routledge
Taylor & Francis Group
270 Madison Avenue
New York, NY 10016

Routledge
Taylor & Francis Group
2 Park Square
Milton Park, Abingdon
Oxon OX14 4RN

© 2007 by Larry Sandberg.
Routledge is an imprint of Taylor & Francis Group, an Informa business

Printed in the United States of America on acid-free paper
10 9 8 7 6 5 4 3 2 1

International Standard Book Number-10: 0-415-97175-6 (Softcover)
International Standard Book Number-13: 978-0-415-97175-1 (Softcover)

No part of this book may be reprinted, reproduced, transmitted, or utilized in any form by any electronic, mechanical, or other means, now known or hereafter invented, including photocopying, microfilming, and recording, or in any information storage or retrieval system, without written permission from the publishers.

Trademark Notice: Product or corporate names may be trademarks or registered trademarks, and are used only for identification and explanation without intent to infringe.

Visit the Taylor & Francis Web site at
http://www.taylorandfrancis.com

and the Routledge Web site at
http://www.routledge-ny.com

Introduction: How to Use This Book

This book is for beginning guitarists who want to learn to play fingerstyle country blues guitar in the styles of Robert Johnson, Big Bill Broonzy, Mance Lipscomb, Lightnin' Hopkins, and Mississippi John Hurt, as well as their followers like Taj Mahal, John Hammond, Jr., Mary Flower, and Eric Clapton. It's unusual in that it's designed to develop awareness of style as well as the basic techniques and concepts, "feel," and thinking that go into this style of playing. For this reason, it can be used along with other books, videos, lessons, and learning approaches, rather than instead of them. Many books and teachers teach you to play by example. This book is intended to get you thinking as well.

This book assumes that you already know your basic chord shapes: the chords on the first two or three frets in the keys of A, C, D, E, and G. It also assumes that you're used to plucking the strings with your fingers rather than a flatpick, or at least that you're willing to do so. That's all you need to be ready to go. Most of the fretting handwork in this book is fairly simple, and takes place on the lower frets of the fingerboard. The emphasis is primarily on the sound and rhythmic security of the picking hand.

This book teaches a creative approach to fingerstyle acoustic guitar blues. Once upon a time, roots musicians learned by watching and playing with older musicians, mostly in family or social situations. In the blues tradition, younger musicians like Robert Johnson got a chance to study firsthand the techniques of older masters like Son House. Sometimes they copied licks. But most important was to strum and sing—that's what came first, keeping the beat going so you could sing your message. The early guitarists of country blues also played a lot for dancing. Again, the beat was primary.

Today, many would-be blues guitarists learn to play out of books, learning from notes or tablature reinforced by a CD, video, or sometimes a live teacher. Often the teacher relies on tablature for his or her teaching (and probably relied on tablature for his or her own learning), and uses a teaching technique based more on showing and rote repetition than on explaining, or on breaking the music down into its component parts. Students become copycats, able to play by rote but lacking the conceptual equipment to create music on their own. Worst of all, since they learn to play notes rather than working outwards from rhythmic gestures in their picking hands, their music lacks rhythmic vitality. The result has been to create two categories of musician. One plays the guitar. The other plays tablature.

This book concentrates mostly on keeping your playing rhythmic and alive. The fretting work is fairly simple—at least, as simple as I can make it while still providing challenges and musical interest—in order to give you a chance to concentrate on learning to play with feeling. In my experience over forty years of teaching the guitar, you can always learn to make your fretting handwork as complex as you care to as time goes on. Learning to play with a compelling rhythmic feeling, if you don't get it at the outset, is much harder to get later on.

By the very nature of book-learning, no book can completely solve this problem. Only practicing and playing live can. But, by presenting a rhythm-based learning method in which the music is broken down into physical and conceptual pieces as part of the learning process, I mean for this book to go a long way. Teachers, I hope, will adopt it as a supplement to their own teaching, using it along with their own materials. Even more, I hope this book will be useful for self-taught or self-teaching students who feel caught on a fogged-in plateau, trapped in the frustrations of rote learning. I hope that by using this book they'll be able to find their way out of the mists, understanding more deeply the music they copy, and learning to use it as a springboard for further exploration and development.

Contents

	Introduction: How to Use This Book	v
Part I	**Preliminaries**	1
	The 12-Bar Blues Form	3
	Reading Chord Charts	4
	Playing in Different Keys	7
Part II	**Touch and Timing**	11
	Track 1: Playing the 12-Bar Blues	13
	Track 2: Key of E	17
	Track 3: Basic Blues in A: Variation	18
	Track 4: Key of C	20
	Track 5: Turnarounds	21
	Track 6: Key of G	24
	Track 7: Singing the Blues	25
	Track 8: Key of D	27
	Track 9: Four Different Turnarounds	28
	Track 10: Thumping the Bass	31
	Track 11: Moving Around the A7 Shape	34
	Track 12: Moving Around the D7 Shape	37
	Tracks 13–14: More Rhythms	38
	Tracks 15–16: Rhythm 2	40
	Tracks 17–18: Rhythm 3	40
	Tracks 19–20: Rhythm 4	41
	Tracks 21–22: Rhythm 5	41
	Tracks 23–24: Rhythm 6	42
	Tracks 25–26: Rhythm 7	42
	Tracks 27–28: Rhythm 8	43

Part III Playing the Blues — 45

Track 29: Blues in E: Major and Minor — 47
Track 30: Blues in E with Blue Notes and Bending — 49
Track 31: Alternating Bass Notes — 51
Track 32: Blues in G — 52
Track 33: Blues in G with Thumping Alternating Bass — 54
Track 34: Blues in G with Steady Bass — 54
Track 35: Blues in E with Moveable Chord Shapes — 54
Track 36: Funky Blues in D with Bending and Vibrato — 57
Tracks 37–38: Happy Blues in D — 60
Track 39: Working Out A Blues in E — 62
Track 40: Ragtime Blues in C — 62

Recommended Listening — 65

PART I

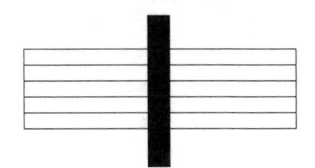

Preliminaries

The 12-Bar Blues Form

The expression *having the blues* to indicate a sad or distressed emotional state has been around for a long time, but sometime around 1900 the word *blues* began to be applied to African-American songs expressing those emotional states.

As a musical term, *blues* has now come to mean a lot of things, including happy songs, sad songs, and songs that we simply think sound "bluesy." Some people even use the term to refer to the entire spectrum of African-American roots music—handy enough when you're sorting CDs into the bin at a record store. When blues achieved commercial success as a musical genre in the 1920s, it was in a musical style that, like Mamie Smith's best-selling "Crazy Blues," we would today describe as having a jazzy take on the pop sounds of the time.

But when musicians sit down with each other today and say, "Let's play some blues," they all know exactly what they mean. They mean, "Let's play in a musical form that takes up 48 beats and has a certain set of chord changes. It reflects a vocal form in which there are three sung lines. There are a few basic variations as to what the chords are and where the changes occur, so we'll sort it out either by agreeing beforehand or just by listening, the first time around, to the senior musician. In other words, let's play some 12-bar blues. Okay, let's go: one, two, three, four...."

That's why it's so easy just to say, "Let's play some blues"—but you have to know what the blues are. It's not that hard to learn the form. That's why it's so popular. But you do have to know it, and you've got to be able to play it without messing up. Otherwise you won't have fun playing with other people, and they for sure won't have fun playing with you.

Even when you play instrumental blues, what underlies that form are words: a verbal structure that consists of a stanza of three sung lines of poetry:

a first line
   (call it line A),
a second line consisting of the words of the first line repeated more or less exactly
   (call it line A repeated), and
a third line, with different words, that answers or extends the thought of the first line
   (call it line B).

Sure, there are variations. Sometimes you'll find different words in all three lines. Sometimes you find the same words in all three lines. But almost all the time, a 12-bar blues has that AAB verse structure. For example:

"You don't know, you don't know, you don't know my mind.
You don't know, you don't know my mind.
When you see me laughin', I'm laughin' just to keep from cryin'."

These words get spread out over 12 *bars* of music.

What is a bar? When musicians write music, we divide up the notes according to the metrical pulse of the music as heard: that is to say, how the beat feels to us when we dance, nod our heads, tap our feet. In most of the music we typically hear around us, we feel the pulse in terms of two-, three-, or four-beat units. Most blues are in four-beat units. In order to make the written music easier to read and feel, we use a vertical line, called a *bar line*, every four beats. These bar lines separate the music into four-beat visual units called *measures*. Properly speaking, "measure" refers to the unit, while "bar" just means the vertical line on the paper. But in casual speech, musicians use "bar" and "measure" interchangeably. (You'll hardly ever hear anyone say "12-measure blues.") So a 12-bar blues is a musical form that takes up 12 units of four beats each. Each of the three sung lines in a blues verse takes up four measures. (When the words don't last for the whole four measures, they get counted out anyway, a few wordless beats for the instruments to play.) And three lines times four measures equals 12 measures or bars, naturally.

Musicians generally refer to one complete 12-bar cycle as a *chorus*, as in, "Sing two choruses and then play an instrumental chorus." (If we were talking about lines of poetry instead of measures of music, though, we'd probably be using the word *stanza* instead. And sometimes you'll hear people say "verse." They all mean the same thing: three AAB lines spread out over 12 measures.)

In a couple of chapters, we'll take a closer look at the relationship between the sung verse and the number of beats it takes up. For the time being, though, let's forget about the words and talk about pure music.

Reading Chord Charts

In addition to having a standard number of beats and measures, the 12-bar blues form has certain set chord changes in certain set places. There are two standard variations, and many that are less common. But for the time being, let's consider only the two main possibilities, in the key of A. Try strumming the following chord changes. Each slash represents one strummed beat, so each chord as indicated lasts for four beats. Use chord shapes you already know—or, if you're not sure, use the following chord shapes.

READING CHORD CHARTS A

A7   D7   E7

Preliminaries

A7	A7 or D7	A7	A7
////	////	////	////
D7	D7	A7	A7
////	////	////	////
E7	D7	A7	A7
////	////	////	////

Congratulations, you've just played a 12-bar blues. Take a look at the chords you've just strummed through. Sure enough, it's easy to see those 12 units of four measures each.

Now take a look at the second measure, where the chart gives you a choice of playing either an A7 or D7. A given blues, throughout its entirety, will go either one way or the other, depending on the shape of its sung melody or the intentions of its composer. In real-life situations, however, it can get confusing. In a blues jam, there can sometimes be chaos at this point as some people go one way, some the other. Generally, on the first time around, all eyes and ears will go to the senior musician, and fingers will follow what he or she does. But even so, there's often some conflict, and even good but poorly rehearsed professionals will mess up from time to time. In this book, the blues we learn will either have one form or the other. Just as in real life, we'll take it on a song-by-song basis. However, you'll notice that most of the examples in this book use the variation that goes to D7, or the equivalent chord in other keys. To my taste, it's a little more interesting that way.

Now let's go back to the chords for the 12-bar blues again, but this time, instead of playing the seventh chords as written, play just plain, ordinary A, D, and E chords. Notice how the music sounds so much less bluesy when you leave out the sevenths. This is because another factor in making blues "bluesy" is using notes like those sevenths, which are called *blue notes*. We'll study them in more detail later. For the time being, just be aware that they exist, and that they're important.

Let's also take a look at some of the ways musicians write out chord changes. A written example of chord changes is called a *chord chart*, or just plain *chart* for short. Charts can take various forms, so it's good to know what they all look like. One is the kind you've just read through above: the chord name is given and the number of beats to be played is placed under it. Another way to indicate the same thing follows:

A7	A7 or D7	A7	
////	////	////	////
D7		A7	
////	////	////	////
E7	D7	A7	
////	////	////	////

Notice that, in the version above, the chord name is not given over every measure, but only when it first occurs. So in the last two measures of the first line, you're actually playing eight beats of A7.

Tracks 1–31 all represent the 12-bar blues in A, but they use different rhythms to express the four-beat units. Listen to any or all of them, but you can hear the four-beat pattern most clearly in Track 1. Like all the tracks, the music begins with four beats counted out on the bass string to set the tempo so you can start playing along in time with the music. Make sure you don't accidentally count the four-beat *pickup*, as it's called, as part of the 12-bar structure.

Another way to write out a chord chart is this:

A7	D7	A7	A7
D7	D7	A7	A7
E7	D7	A7	A7

The above system is fast and easy; it's the way a music teacher might jot down some chords for you in a lesson, or the way a musician might jot down a chord progression for future reference on a piece of scrap paper. But there's nothing here that tells you how many beats to play on each chord—you'd have to know that because someone told you, or from context, or from having heard the song. Or you'd just have to make a guess based on experience, or the way you'd think the song should go.

Finally, there's the strictly formal rhythm chart using staff lines of notated music. It looks like this, and sounds the same as all the other charts you've just read:

12-Bar Blues Chord Chart

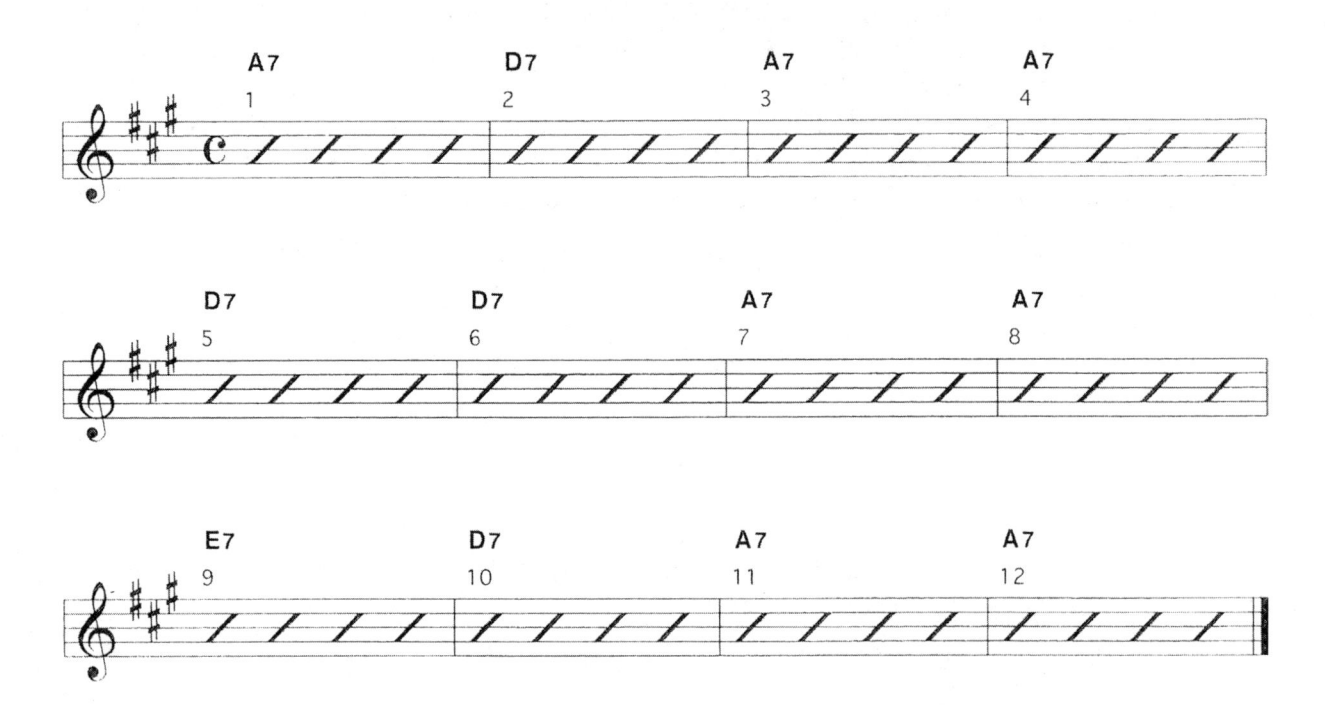

Playing in Different Keys

If you know how to transpose, you can skip this chapter. If you find this chapter hard or boring, you can skip it for now and come back to it later. At some point in your musical career, you're going to discover that not knowing how to change keys or figure out chord relationships is a severe disability. When this happens, you'll realize that you need to come back to this chapter. That will be the time, and you'll know it.

The first section of this book consists of examples drawn from the key of A. As we've seen, the blues chords in the key of A are A, D, and E, with or without the sevenths. Notice the numerical relationship between the letters. Starting on A and counting A as "one," the D is four letters higher than A; similarly, the E is five letters higher than A. In music, the distance between notes is called an *interval*. A to D would be an interval of a *fourth*, A to E would be called an interval of a *fifth*, and so on. In traditional notation, musicians use roman numerals to indicate this relationship: I, IV, and V. (In recent use, though, it has also become acceptable to use regular arabic numerals.) When you indicate chords or notes in their abstract numerical relationships this way, it's said that you're referring to them by *degree*. The word *degree* comes from the Latin word for *step*.

The technique of moving music from one key to another is called *transposition*, and that's what we'll be doing in the following chord charts. The idea is that the entire piece of music becomes higher or lower, but the degree relationships between notes and chords stay the same.

If you have a good mathematical mind, better than most people's, transposition is very easy. Other musicians get fast and accurate at transposition because they have to, no matter how hard or easy they find it. Studio musicians and vocal accompanists—especially church musicians—often have to move keys higher or lower in order to suit the singers' voices. The rest of us are often slower, sometimes needing to count up chord changes on our fingers, or puzzling them out with pencil and paper. Whether you turn out to be a runner or crawler depends on your native aptitude and on how much transposing you actually wind up doing in your musical life. Don't be embarrassed about crawling. But whether you run, walk, or crawl to get there, understanding transposition is a goal that most musicians need to attain, especially for playing with others. Look over the following charts. They all represent 12-bar blues:

Degree System

I7	IV7	I7	I7
IV7	IV7	I7	I7
V7	IV7	I7	I7

Key of A

A7	D7	A7	A7
D7	D7	A7	A7
E7	D7	A7	A7

Key of C

C7	F7	C7	C7
F7	F7	C7	C7
G7	F7	C7	C7

Key of D

D7	G7	D7	D7
G7	G7	D7	D7
A7	G7	D7	D7

Key of E

E7	A7	E7	E7
A7	A7	E7	E7
B7	A7	E7	E7

Key of G

G7	C7	G7	G7
C7	C7	G7	G7
D7	D7	G7	G7

We've learned that moving music from one key to another is called transposition, and that's what we've just done.

Fingerstyle blues guitarists do most of their work in the keys of A, C, D, E, and G, and that's why I've given charts for them. Other keys, including minor keys, are less usual in traditional blues. Though they're perfectly fine and very interesting, they're outside the basic repertoire and won't be included in this book.

One of the peculiarities of the guitar is that different keys offer radically different sounds, as well as different fingering challenges. This depends in part on the nature of the chord shapes that are physically possible to play in each key, and partly on the way those chord shapes relate to the open strings. To some extent, the difference in the sounds and physical possibilities of different keys is reflected on all musical instruments, even in the combinations of sounds and instruments available in a symphony orchestra. But this is especially true of the guitar. It's both a limitation and one of the qualities that makes the guitar so interesting to play.

As you strum through the chord charts below, even using simple beginner's chords, you may begin even now to notice this quality about guitar keys. You may notice, for example, that chords like A7, D7, and E7 have an extra amount of ring and sustain coming from the open strings, but that chords like C7 and F7 don't. You may notice, especially if you're a beginner, that a basic F chord, which is hard enough for beginners, is still easier than an F7, so you may be tempted to play just a plain F instead of the F7. To some extent, you're fudging and being lazy when you choose to do this. On the other hand, it's a very natural response to the guitar. It might lead you to develop a personal style, a feature of which is that, when you play the basic first-fret chord shapes, you prefer Fs to F7s. Likewise, in the key of E, a basic B7 shape is pretty easy for beginners to play. On the other hand, beginners rarely use a B chord, since it has to be played either with a difficult barred fingering or only partially, on a few strings.

When you learn to copy someone else's music or to play a classical piece, you're obliged to master whatever challenges that music demands of you. When you're making your own musical decisions, you'll be working toward your own style based on very simple choices, like whether you prefer an F or an F7. That's how the great guitarists get their distinctively original sound.

FURTHER WORK 1. Don't try to assimilate all these keys, or all the information from this chapter, in one big gulp as if you're cramming for an exam. Learning music doesn't work that way, especially with this kind of material. Play with all these examples over a long period of time, going back to them even as you proceed into later chapters of this book.

FURTHER WORK 2. All the preceding examples are based on a first line that goes:

I7   IV7   I7   I7

Be aware that many blues can instead go like this in the first line:

I7   I7   I7   I7

Go back and work in all five keys using this structure for the first four measures. Also notice how this exercise is not only about blues structure, but also about getting you to think of translating the abstract roman numerals into actual chord letters.

In the coming chapters, we'll be working on a variety of techniques in the key of A. As you go along, please make it your business to apply them to the 12-bar blues chord progression in the other four keys as well. I'll give you some help with this, but you'll need to be working on your own as well.

PART II

Touch and Timing

In this section, we'll be working mostly to develop a secure sense of timing with the 12-bar blues chord changes, expressed with a robust, rhythmically secure picking and strumming technique. We'll also explore a few concepts relating to how chord shapes can be moved around on the fingerboard. The written examples will be in the key of A, but the CD examples will encourage you to play in the other keys as well.

Track 1: Playing the 12-Bar Blues

This will be a wordy chapter. I'll be talking here not only about the music in Track 1, but also about some of the ways to use the book. In later chapters the music-to-words ratio will be higher.

Let's begin by listening to the example in Track 1. As with all the musical examples on the CD for this book, the guitar counts four beats to set the tempo (the pickup)—a sort of *ready, set, go* to let you know when, and at what pace, the song will start.

As with most of the musical examples in this book, I'll give you the chord shapes you'll need to use in order to finger the notation or tablature for each track. Please make yourself familiar with these shapes, and get used to using them in making chord changes, before you try to play the example. You'll notice that in this example, and many others, the notation will not require you to play all the notes that you finger as part of the chord shape. It doesn't matter: *Finger the complete shape anyway.* I'd like you to do this for several reasons. One is that blues, folk, jazz, and other improvising guitarists, as opposed to traditional classical musicians, usually think in terms of standard chord shapes rather than individual notes. Another is that having *all* possible notes of the chord under your fingers will help you see possibilities for variation and improvisation. And the third reason, which we'll look at a few tracks further on, is that having the complete chords under your fingers will give you the option of getting a fuller sound by brushing across extra strings, even when they're not specifically notated, in order to get a fuller sound.

PREP WORK. Before we actually play the musical examples in this book, I'll often give you some information or exercises to help prepare your mind or fingers for the piece. The chords you'll need for this example are:

Track 1 Chord Chart

A7   A7   D7   E7

Keep these chord shapes in mind—or, rather, in your fingers—as you play the following example. In it, you'll be plucking a steady series of bass notes, one per beat, with your thumb. Along with the first of every four bass notes, you'll also be plucking a chord on the high strings.

The bass notes essentially fill the role of a drummer, providing a beat that helps keep the time steady. It also provides a reference for the ear to follow the chord changes. You'll be plucking the open A string when you play the A7 chord, the open D string when you play the D7 chord, and the open E string when you play the E7 chord.

While your thumb is keeping time with the steady bass notes in Track 1, your picking fingers will be playing a three-note chord on the high strings along with the first of every four bass notes. How you execute these notes is up to you. Many fingerstyle guitarists playing blues, folk, or Americana styles prefer to use only their thumb and two fingers.

Wait a minute: that's *two* fingers being asked to play *three* strings. There are several ways you can handle it. You can use three fingers, as a fair number of guitarists do, especially those who like to use bare fingers. (Players who prefer wearing fingerpicks often find using the ring finger to be awkward.)

Another way to play the three strings is to use a brushing motion in your picking move, so one finger sets two strings into motion. (Probably you'll find it most natural to use your index finger to play the second and third strings.)

Finally, you can do what most of the old-time blues guitarists did: You can strum those three high notes all with your index finger as it moves in an upward pinching motion along with the downward-moving thumb. Plucking individual strings with two or three fingers will give you a clean sound. Brushing up with the index finger gives you, well, a brushy sound, and also a louder one. I'll be playing one way or the other on the various examples on the CD. See if you can guess from the sound which technique I'm using, but make your own decisions and go for a sound and style of your own.

Track 1. Basic Blues in A

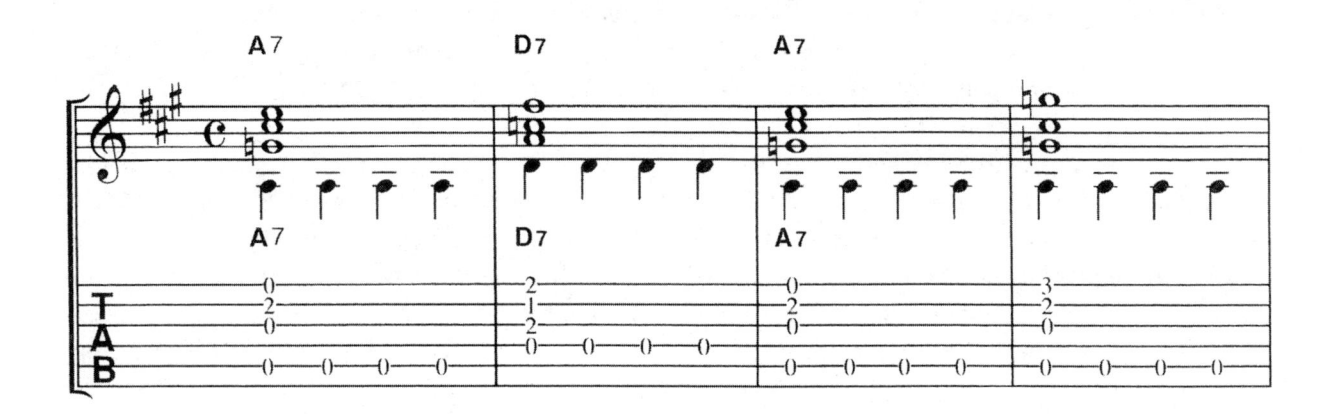

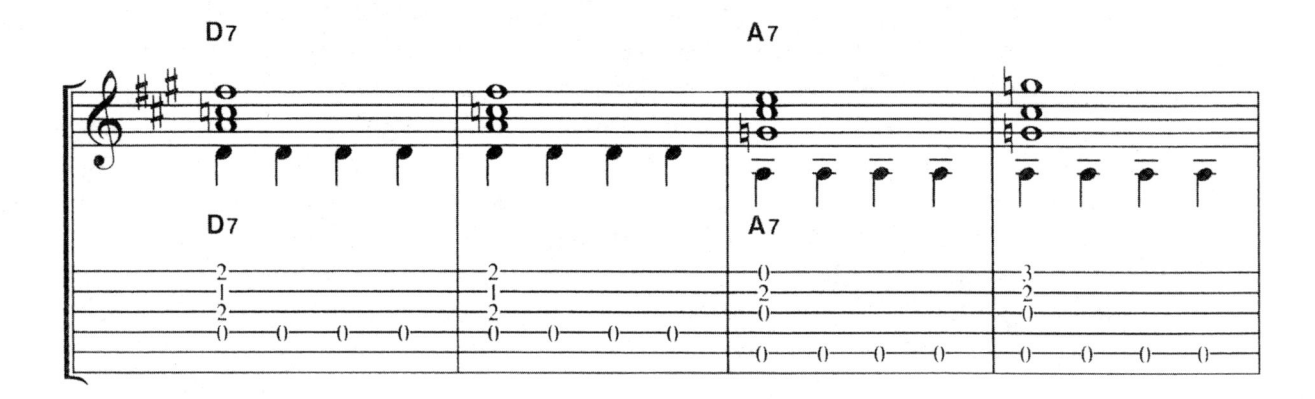

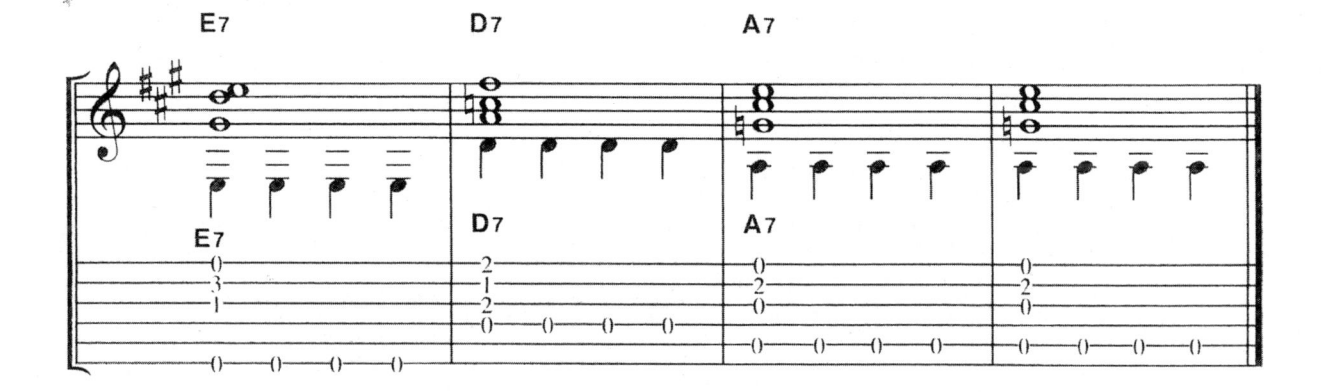

FURTHER WORK 1. You've already encountered a "further work" section in the preceding chapter. Along with the musical examples in this book—to be learned by rote—I'll also be asking you to figure out on your own some ways of extending what you've already learned. In most cases, this is much harder work that just following an example. I'm hoping that it will help train to make your own choices. In many cases, the "further work" that I suggest will be very much as if you were to ask yourself, "What if I were to do something different, to experiment, to depart from the rote example by using my own imagination?"

Let's apply this way of thinking to the steady bass notes you've learned to play in this example: the A string for the A7 chord, the D string for the D7 chord, and the E string for the E7. In most of the examples in this book, the bass note I give you to play will be the same note that the chord is named after—what musicians call the *tonic note* of the chord. In the absence of any other consideration, these are the safest, surest, more sensible notes to play; besides being a good habit to get into, this practice helps establish the intended "meaning" of the chords as you and your audiences hear them, for the human musical mind tends to hear and analyze chords from the lowest note up.

On the other hand, there's no reason why you should have to be a safe, sensible creature of habit all the time. In fact, it might be bad for you. So once you learn the piece with the sensible bass notes, try playing others. Generally speaking, in fingerpicking guitar (and this also is a rule that's made to be broken) the lowest-sounding three strings are thumb territory and the highest three strings are finger territory. So for the bass note, you've got the fourth, fifth, and sixth strings to play with. (Potentially, at least—you may have to limit your choices depending on whether a given bass string is part of the chord shape you're playing, or whether a given open string sounds good with the chord shape.) The way you do this is to ask: "What if…?" For example, what if I play the fifth string on the E7 chord, instead of the sixth string as written? Does it fit? Do I like it better or worse? Do I like it all the time or some of the time? What if I try the fourth string? Are the bass note police going to show up at my door and take me away in cuffs? Or am I in fact going to find out something new, on my own?

In the case of the example you've just learned, there are some "what ifs" that can apply to the way you play the high strings as well. What if you only play two of the three notes that are written in the example? Does it sound weaker? Or leaner and meaner? How do you like the sound if you play only the first and second strings? Or only the second and third strings? How about experimenting with sound by randomly going back and forth between these two pairs of strings? What if you did that?

You don't have to wait to become a virtuoso to start thinking creatively. Track 1 is a pretty easy piece of music, once you get comfortable with keeping that bass steady. Even so, it offers creative possibilities. At the point that you start exploring the "what ifs," you're starting to create your own original arrangement of my piece. Music doesn't have to be hard; only suckers fall in that trap. But original is original. So by all means, explore the "further work" I give you, but also try to come up with some "what ifs" of your own.

You'll have to figure out how you learn best. Some people will prefer to explore the "further work" before moving on to the next track. Others will move on sooner, while still fooling around with the previous tracks. It's up to you. With imagination, you can spread it out over a lifetime.

Touch and Timing

FURTHER WORK 2. The CD examples are played at fairly slow tempos. As you master each track, learn to play them at faster tempos as well. Best yet, learn to play them at several different tempos: slow, medium, and fast, until you figure out what sounds right to you. (You can get a sense of rightness by listening to other players.) Bear in mind two important things. First, don't try to play anything faster than you can. Otherwise, you'll be practicing playing sloppily, and if playing sloppily is what you practice, then it's what you'll get good at. Second, notice how much music out there actually isn't very fast. In fact, there's a tendency for amateurs to play faster than the pros do.

FURTHER WORK 3. Here, and in other chapters, go back and learn to play what you have learned in other keys than A. If necessary, consult the earlier "Playing in Different Keys" section to review the 12-bar chord progression for other keys. For most chord shapes, keep the steady bass going on the lowest fingered or open bass string that belongs to the chord. If something sounds wrong to you, then experiment with other bass strings until you've found a steady bass note you're happy with. However, to help you on your way, Tracks 1, 3, 5, and 7 (all in A) are each followed by a related track in a different key.

Track 2: Key of E

Track 2 is for CD work by ear, without consulting any written music. It's the 12-bar pattern for the key of E, using the following chord shapes. For bass notes, play:

    Sixth string for the E7 chord
    Fifth string for the A7 and B7 chords

Track 2 Chord Chart

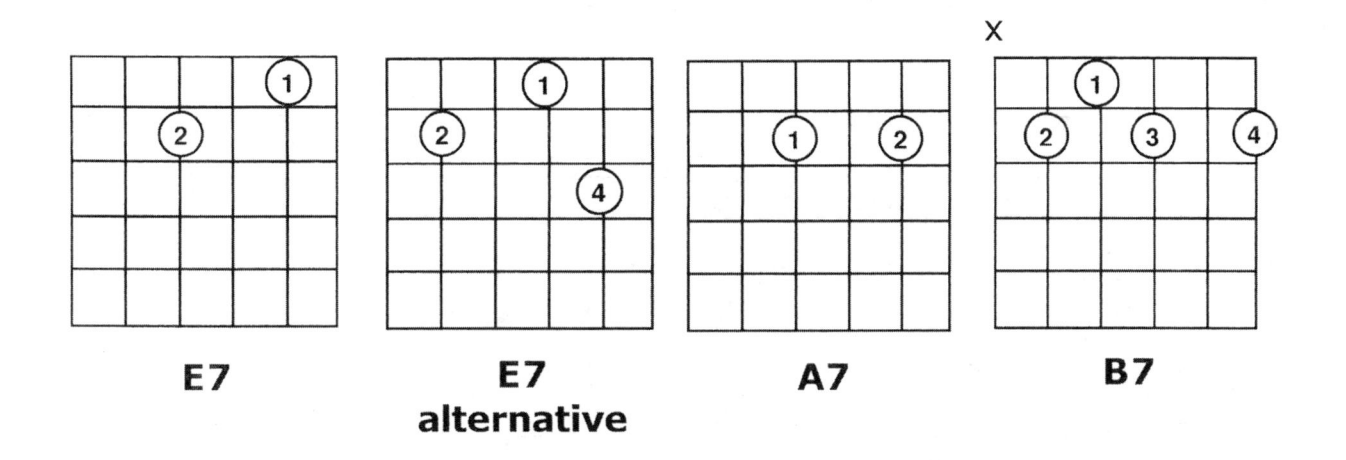

E7   **E7 alternative**   **A7**   **B7**

Track 3: Basic Blues in A: Variation

If you've got Track 1 down, Track 3 should be pretty easy. It's almost the same, playing the high notes of a chord against a steady thumb beat. But this time, instead of playing the high notes once every four thumb strokes, let's play them once every four thumb strokes. The chord shapes are identical to those used in Track 1.

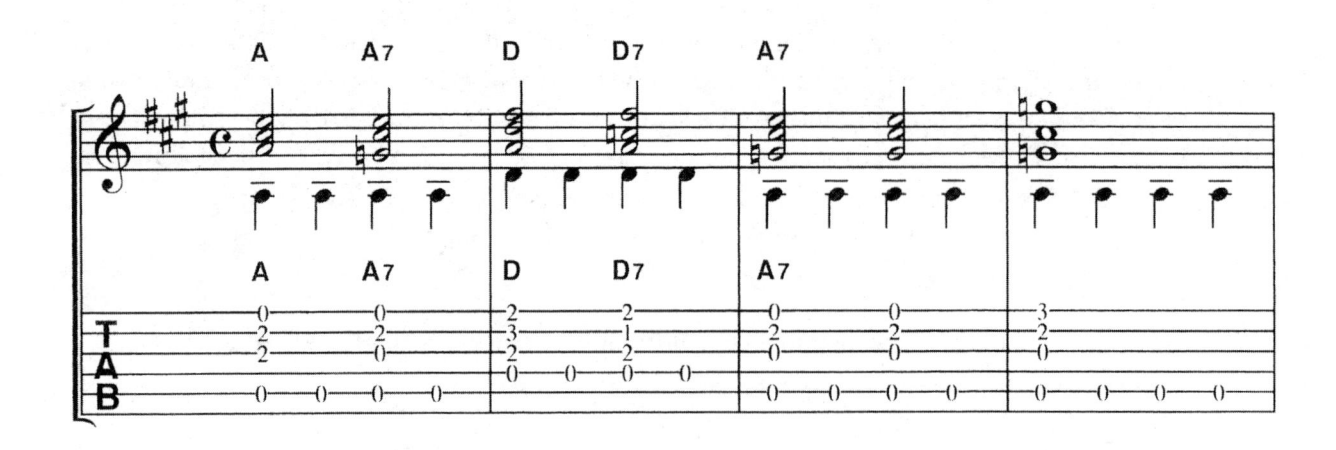

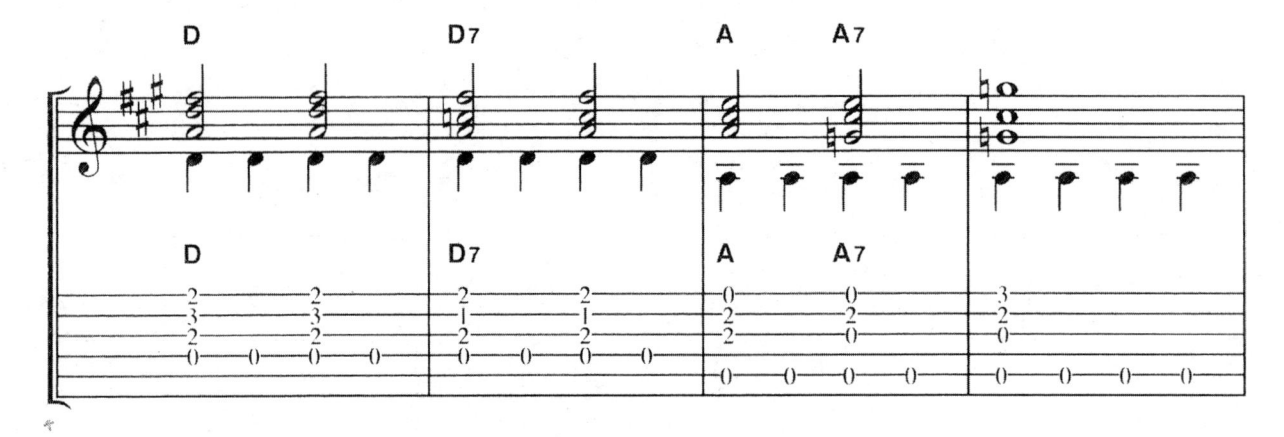

Track 3. Basic Blues in A: Variation

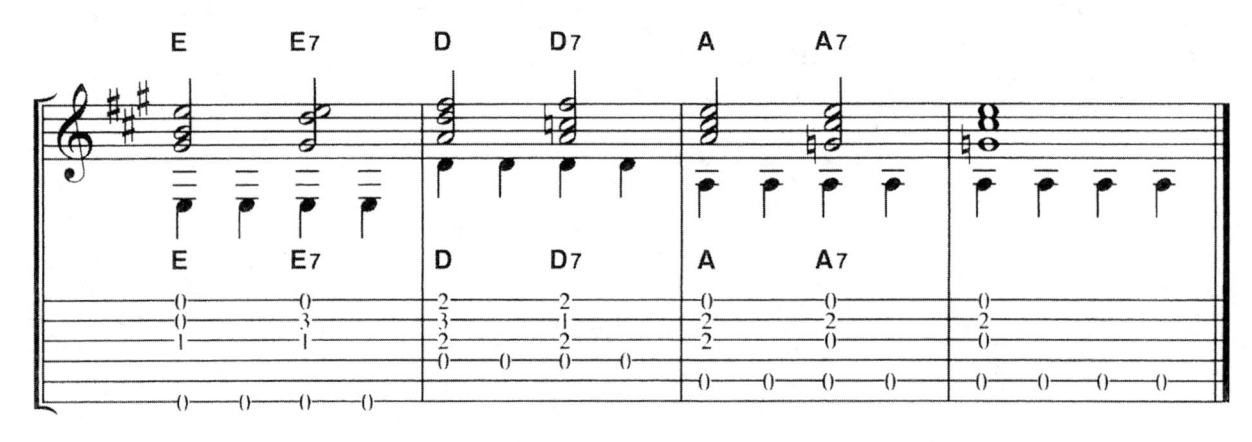

FURTHER WORK. The most important thing in this style of blues playing is to keep that thumb beat steady. What if you tried to put the high notes of the chord in different places? As you experiment, you'll find that some of your results are easy and some are hard. Some will sound pleasing; some may sound lopsided. Make your own decisions about which results you'll reject and which ones you'll accept and incorporate into your style as it develops, because that's what you're doing right now, even at the beginning: developing your own style. You learn and earn your own style by making choices at every step of the way about which paths you'll follow and which you won't.

In order to explore the following possibilities, try practicing at first only on one chord, then going back and forth between any two of the three chords. After you've done this for a while and have gotten secure with each picking pattern, then apply it to the complete 12-bar blues progression. Here are some ideas:

- Play the high notes with the second and fourth thumb strokes, instead of the first and second.
- Play the high notes only on the second beat of each measure, or only on the third, or the fourth.
- Play one pattern on the A7 measures, another only on the D7 measures, and another only on the E7 measure.
- Vary the patterns every two or four measures.
- Try to come up with some other variations on your own.

Track 4: Key of C

Try playing what you've learned from Track 3 in the key of C, using the following chords:

TRACK 4 CHORD CHART

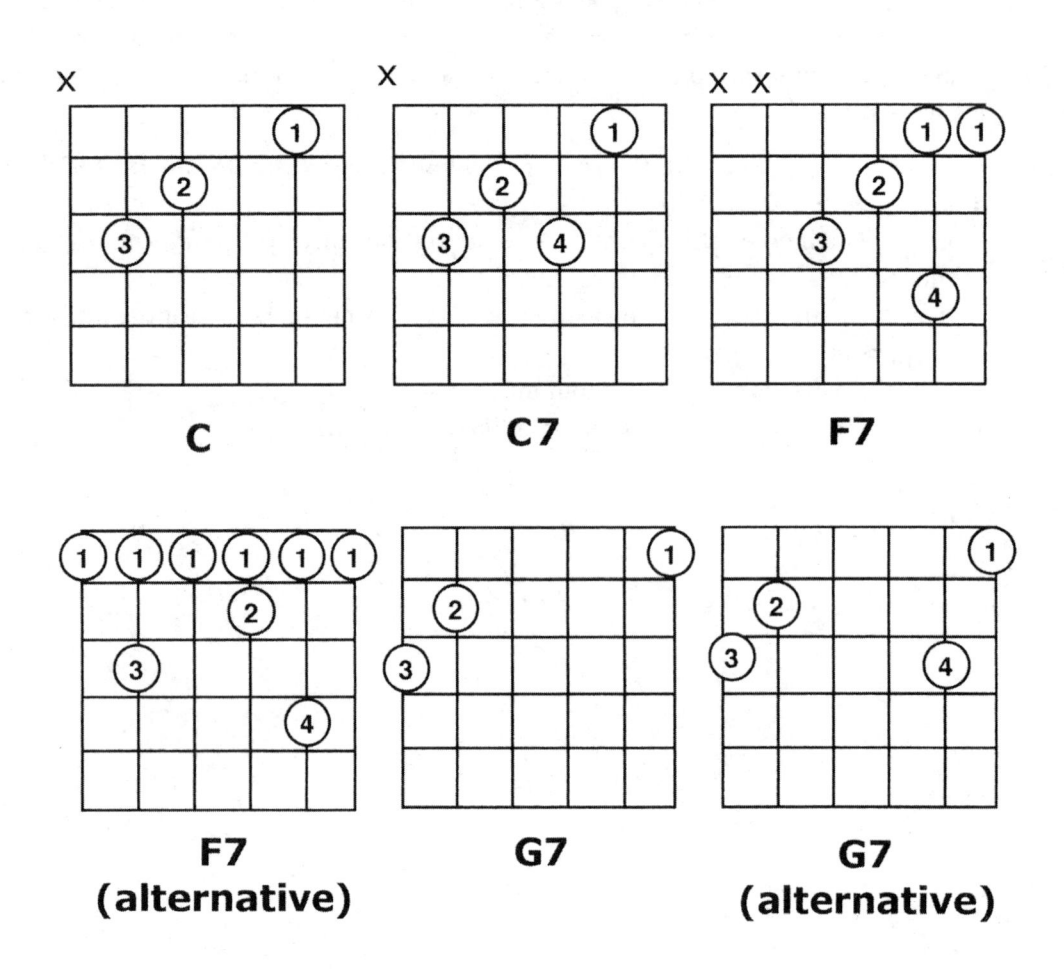

C **C7** **F7**

F7 (alternative) **G7** **G7 (alternative)**

Use the following strings for the steady bass:

C7 chord: fifth string
F7 and G7 chords: sixth string

Track 5: Turnarounds

Before we go any further, let's get used to one more important feature of the 12-bar blues structure: the *turnaround*. Go back to the section on "The 12-Bar Blues Form" and look at the chord charts. A blues chorus in the key of A typically begins with at least four beats of A (or A7) and ends with eight beats of A (or A7). Sometimes, when you play one chorus after another, it can be hard to keep track of where the ending A7 ends and the beginning A7 ends.

To solve this problem, blues musicians will insert a *turnaround* as a signal to separate the last beat of one chorus from the first beat of the next. A turnaround is anything you do to help signal the end of the chorus. In a band, it could be as simple as some extra strong pounding on the drums, or some loud repeated notes from the bass player, or the lead singer thrusting her arm into the air if she senses that the band is falling apart behind her. But the most ordinary way to signal a turnaround is to put a chord change on the last few beats of the chorus. Here's an ordinary 12-bar blues, four beats to each chord:

A7	D7	A7	A7
D7	D7	A7	A7
E7	D7	A7	**A7**

Instead of playing the above, you could play an E7 chord as the turnaround:

A7	D7	A7	A7
D7	D7	A7	A7
E7	D7	A7	**E7**

And you'd keep on playing this over and over until you got to the end of the song, when there were no more choruses to turn around to. Then, instead of playing that final E7, you'd end on A or A7. Track 5 shows how it's written and sounds.

Track 5. Basic Blues in A: Variation with Turnaround

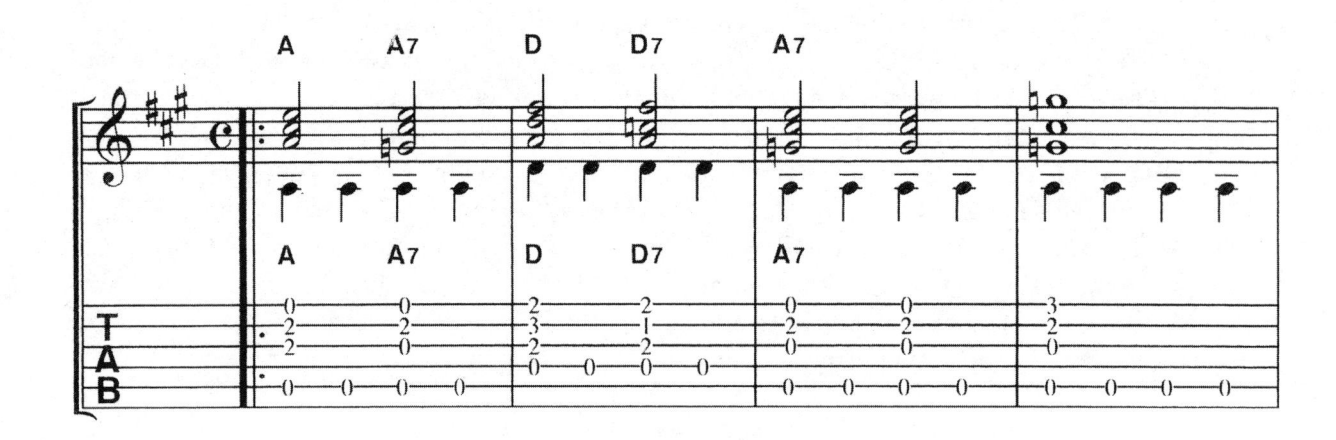

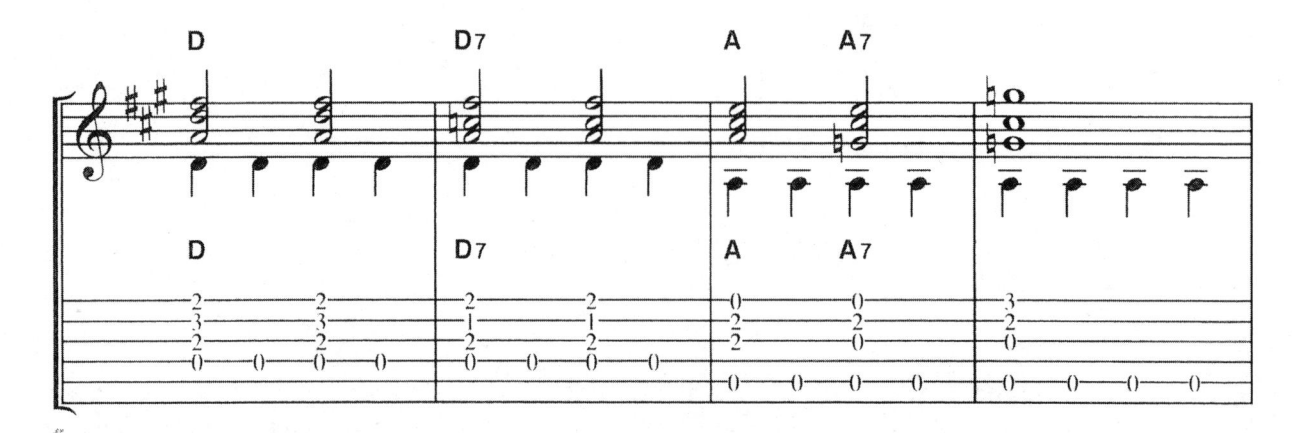

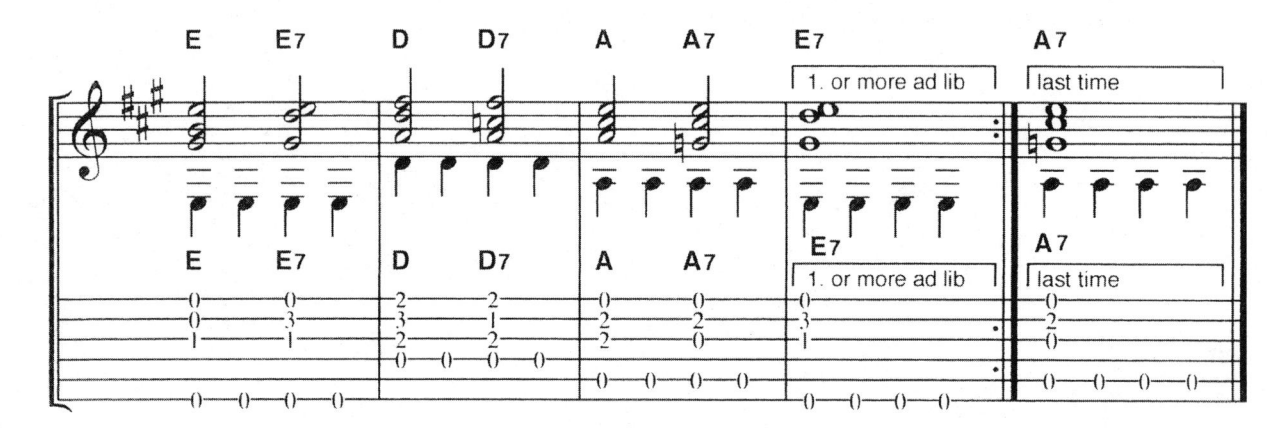

FURTHER WORK. A problem with writing a blues book full of notated examples, and putting them on a CD, is that it's important to conserve space. Therefore many of the tracks consist of a 12-bar blues only once through, with no need or space for a turnaround. For this reason, I'm going to ask you, as you learn the examples, to play them as several continuous choruses and put in the turnaround yourself, just as musicians do in real life. Later on, as we get past the preliminaries, we'll learn some more turnarounds. In the meantime, as you listen to blues (or many other genres, like country), try to take notice of how musicians use turnarounds—various chord and rhythm changes—to signal the end of one chorus and the "lead-in" (transition) to the next.

Also note that Track 5 uses the same rhythm as Track 3. Go back to the suggestions in the "Further Work" for Track 3 and incorporate them into your new way of playing blues with the turnaround.

Finally, let me remind you again that the examples are played pretty slowly. Try also to play them a little faster, a lot faster, and also even more slowly. Very slow blues can be beautiful to listen to and to play, and you may wind up discovering what experienced musicians already know: that playing very slowly can be harder than playing fast.

Track 6: Key of G

Here's what we learned in Track 5, but now set in the key of G using the following chord shapes:

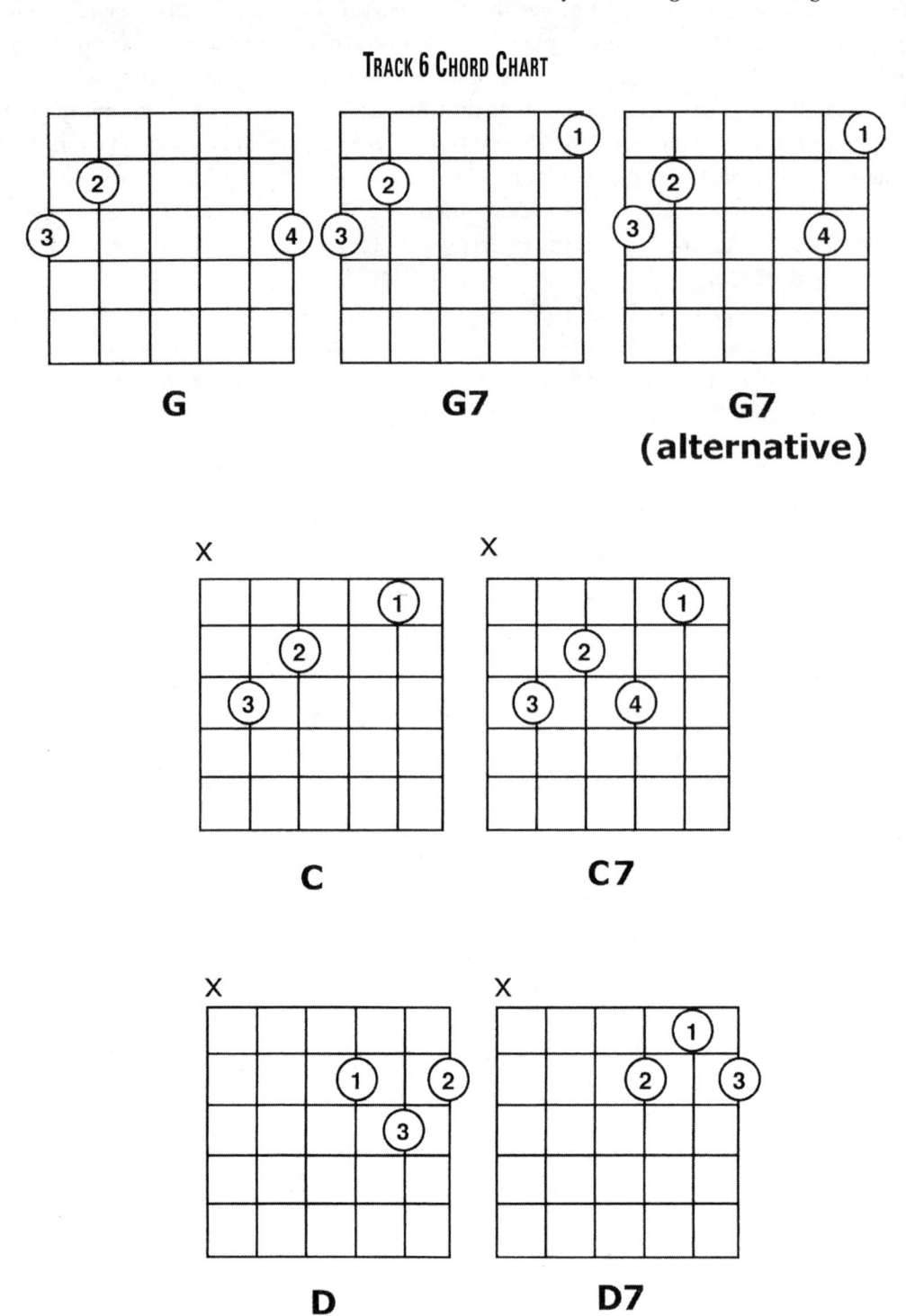

Track 6 Chord Chart

G   **G7**   **G7 (alternative)**

C   **C7**

D   **D7**

Use the following strings for the steady bass notes:

G7 chord: sixth string
C7 chord: fifth string
D7 chord: fourth string

Track 7: Singing the Blues

This book is about playing the guitar, but it's not really possible to understand the blues without having a sense of blues singing and the way words work in the 12-bar structure. Even if you don't sing, listen to singers. And even if you don't sing, sing anyway. Instrumentalists who (quite rightly) wouldn't open their mouths in public will often sing in the basement in order to please themselves, help the learning process, and add emotional and musical meaning to the experience of playing the blues.

PREP WORK. Go back to "The 12-Bar Blues Form" and refresh yourself on the first few paragraphs dealing with the verse structure of the blues.

Now listen to Track 7 to hear, in the first chorus, how the words of a typical line fall against the beat and chord structure. However, in the second chorus (note that there's a turnaround), I've sung, to the beat of my vocal abilities, exactly the same words but in a different rhythm. The way I place the syllables in the first chorus is pretty ordinary. The second chorus is somewhat exaggerated, though. Only a deliberately stylized singer would phrase this way, or an instrumental soloist. I could especially imagine a sax player expressing the melody this way, or a singer who was thinking in terms of a sax solo.

Track 7. Accompaniment for Singing the Blues

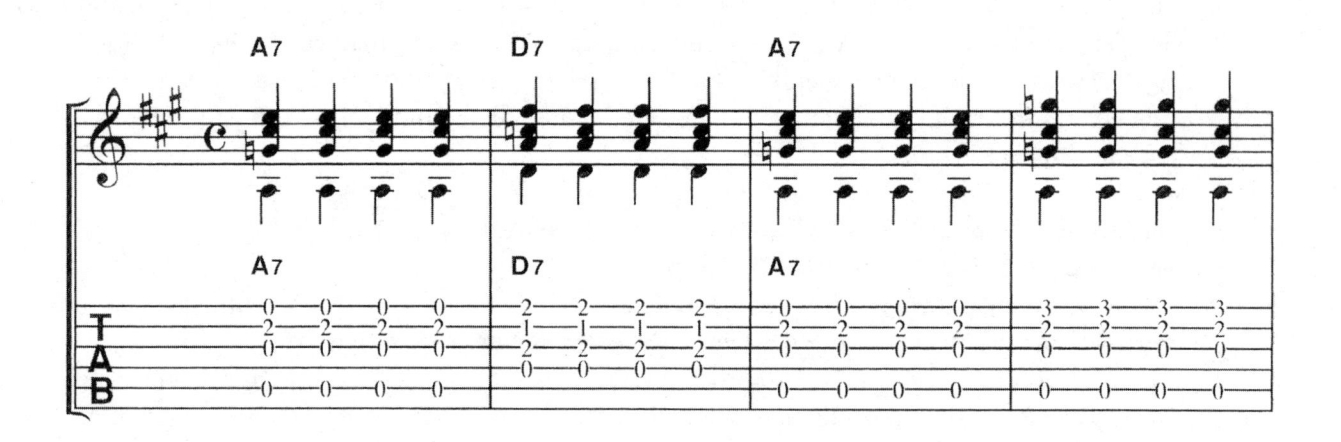

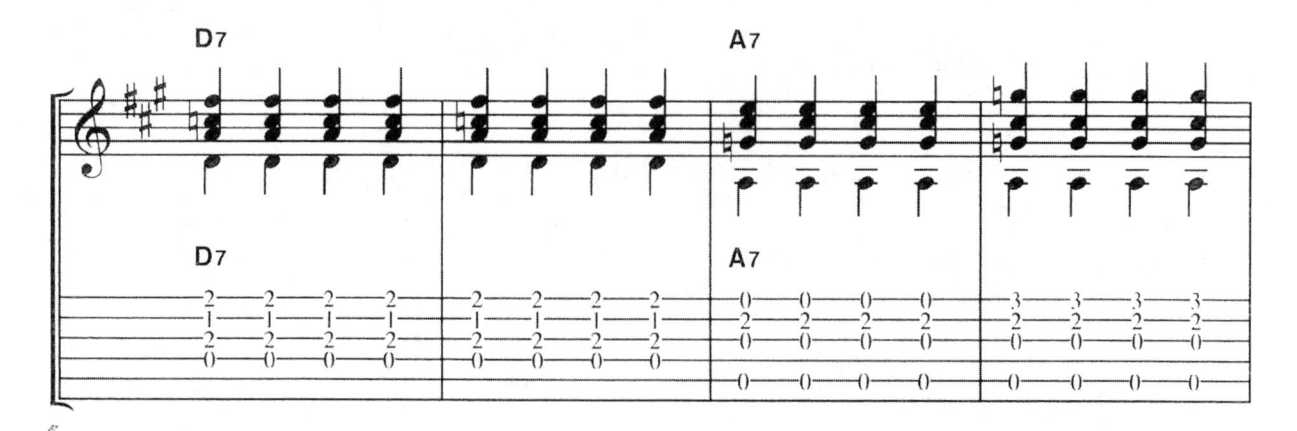

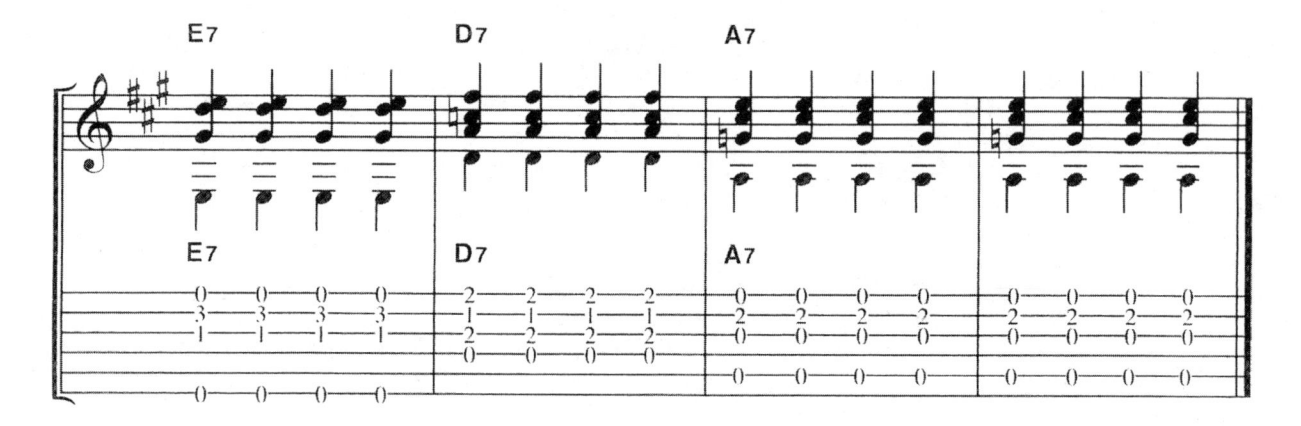

There's an important lesson to be learned from the differences between the phrasing of the first and second choruses: You can't always depend on the lyrics of a blues song to tell you when to change the chords. Many, perhaps most, 12-bar blues lyrics get sung approximately the way I've sung the first chorus: they end about five beats from the end of each four-measure line, leaving a little room for an instrumentalist to fill the space when the vocalist is done—but not always. So, in order to be a good blues player, *don't* follow the singer. Follow the abstract structure of the 12-bar blues just the way you've learned it.

Once upon a time, in the bayous, the backwoods, and cotton fields, blues players were all over the place, rhythmically. Sometimes it was by accident, other times deliberate. The players created 11-bar, 14-bar, even 13-and-a-half bar blues—and they sounded great. Those days are over now, except when someone is going for an unusual or historical effect. People play their blues in the 12-bar form almost all the time.

FURTHER WORK. Learning how to sing the blues can be an important part of learning how to play the blues. Not being the greatest singer hasn't stopped me and it shouldn't stop you; so wait for your friends and family to leave, get down to the basement, and start singing. Listen to CDs, sing along, and learn the words. If you have trouble with vocal range in a given key, then change it, or use a capo.

Track 8: Key of D

Track 8 on the CD uses the rhythm from Track 7, now played in the key of D with the following chord shapes:

Track 8 Chord Chart

D7   **G7**   **A7**

Use the following strings for the steady bass notes:

D7 chord: fourth string
G7 chord: fifth string
A7 chord: sixth string

Track 9: Four Different Turnarounds

PREP WORK. If necessary, review Track 5. Also learn the following chord shapes:

Track 9 Chord Chart

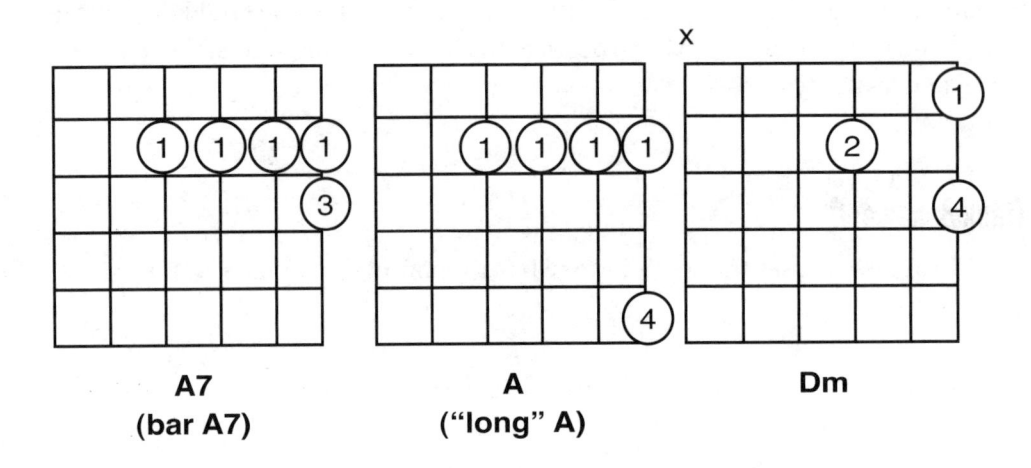

A7
(bar A7)

A
("long" A)

Dm

Practice going back and forth between these two chords. You can see why the long A chord shape is called that. If you're having trouble making the stretch with your pinky, try placing your thumb a little further down on the back of the neck.

Also, note that most of the time guitarists find it easier to play the barred A7 with the index finger making the bar and the third (ring) finger making the high note on the third fret. However, when you're going back and forth between the long A and the barred A7, you may find it easier to use the second (middle) finger to play the high note instead of the third finger.

As you listen to lots of blues, you'll discover that there are dozens, if not hundreds, of turnarounds. So far, we've only used one. Back in Track 5 we used four beats of E7 in the key of A; its transposed equivalent in Track 6 was a D7 in the key of G. Here are four more turnarounds. Each line of the written music below represents the last sung line—the last four bars—of a 12-bar blues:

1. The first turnaround goes to the E7 chord for only two beats, instead of the four beats we learned in Track 3.
2. The second turnaround takes up the last two measures. Instead of going just to an E7, it goes

```
A       D7      A       E7
//      //      //      //
```

3. The third turnaround also takes up two measures, but with more and faster chord changes before it finally turns around on E7. It goes

```
A     A7    D     D7    A      E7
/     /     /     /     //     //
```

4. The fourth turnaround doesn't use a chord change at all to turn around. Instead, it uses a rhythm change at the end of the 12-bar chorus to signal that the next chorus is about to begin. Solo guitarists don't use this kind of turnaround too much; you're more likely to hear it in a band, because it's a drummer's trick. You'll hear from the example that, even though there's no chord change at the end of the chorus, the turnaround to the next chorus is made perfectly clear by the way the rhythm doubles up. Sometimes a rhythmic and a chord change will be combined. Try this yourself. For example, instead of staying on A over the last four beats of the chorus, play an E7 chord at the point where the rhythm changes.

Written out, the four turnarounds look like this:

TRACK 9. FOUR DIFFERENT TURNAROUNDS (EACH LINE OF MUSIC REPRESENTS THE LAST FOUR BARS OF A 12-BAR BLUES IN **A**)

The arrangement for a given blues song will generally use the same turnaround in every chorus. In a quick rehearsal, musicians will usually agree beforehand on what the turnaround will be. In an informal jam, musicians will usually follow the lead of the senior player, and sometimes it can be a while before everyone gets together on the same turnaround. I once got on stage to play an unrehearsed blues with another guitarist, and at the end of the first chorus we each played a different turnaround. At the end of the second chorus, we each played the turnaround the other had used the first time. We've been friends ever since.

FURTHER WORK. The written examples represent the entire final four measures of a 12-bar blues, but remember that the turnaround itself only takes up the last two, four, or eight beats. First master the four turnarounds as written, just practicing the four measures. Then incorporate them into a series of consecutive 12-bar blues choruses. As you get used to them, try varying the rhythms as much as you can. Also try inventing some different rhythms for the fourth turnaround. (Remember: Any rhythmic variation that makes it clear when the chorus ends will do the job.) Finally, try using the rhythm of the fourth turnaround together with the chord changes of the first three turnarounds.

As I said in Track 5, the examples in this book sometimes take up only one chorus, so make it your business to choose among these turnarounds and incorporate them on your own. Think for yourself. To encourage you, you'll also notice that a few of the tracks are written out as only one chorus, without a turnaround, but when you play along with the CD, you'll find that there are several choruses, separated by one or another of the turnarounds you've just learned. This is a deliberate tactic to make you listen and learn and think things out on your own.

Track 10: Thumping the Bass

There are two basic approaches to playing blues guitar (and some other genres as well). One is to execute the notes you wish to play cleanly, picking each note clearly and precisely. The other is to play with a broader, more abandoned stroke, brushing across several strings with your thumb or finger. This gives you more drive and a more robust sound, but sounds less polished and precise.

When you play music out of a book, there's a tendency to focus on the individual notes on the paper before your eyes and to tend to think more about executing the notes cleanly than about playing with rhythmic force and authority. It's inevitable. The people who become good guitarists by learning out of books are the ones who get beyond this stage and play the guitar rather than the notes. I'd like to devote Track 10 to helping you accomplish this. It's only a start, but perhaps it will get you thinking and feeling on the right track.

The written example for Track 10 looks a lot like that for Track 2, with an important exception. Instead of indicating a cleanly played single thumb note in the steady bass, I've indicated a pair of notes. To play them, swipe robustly with your thumb across the two strings indicated. Make a strong, wide stroke, and don't worry if you wind up running your thumb across a third string as well.

Take a similar approach to the high notes. Play all three of them with a broad, strong upward stroke of the index finger. Although the written music asks you to play three notes, don't worry if you only play two, or if your stroke is so broad that you actually play four. Play the beat, instead of worrying about how exactly you play the written score. Use the score as a cue for when to move your picking fingers, not as a literal representation of exactly which notes to hit.

Finally, note that the strong thumping sound on the CD comes not only from the strength of the stroke but also from *muting* the strings. (Some guitarists also call this *damping* or *dampening* the strings.) Different guitarists mute the strings in different ways. Watch videos or live performances and you'll see the following techniques, sometimes more than one in the playing of a single guitarist:

- Touching the thumb back onto a bass string to silence it once it has been played.
- Lowering the flat of the picking hand onto the strings to silence them.
- Rotating the pinky side of the picking hand onto the strings to silence them.
- Briefly releasing the pressure of the chording hand on the strings to silence them.
- Briefly moving the chording fingers onto open strings in order to silence them.

Listen for the way the sound of the strings is cut short in Track 6 in order to emphasize the thumping quality of the strum.

Touch and Timing

TRACK 10. BLUES WITH THUMPING BASS

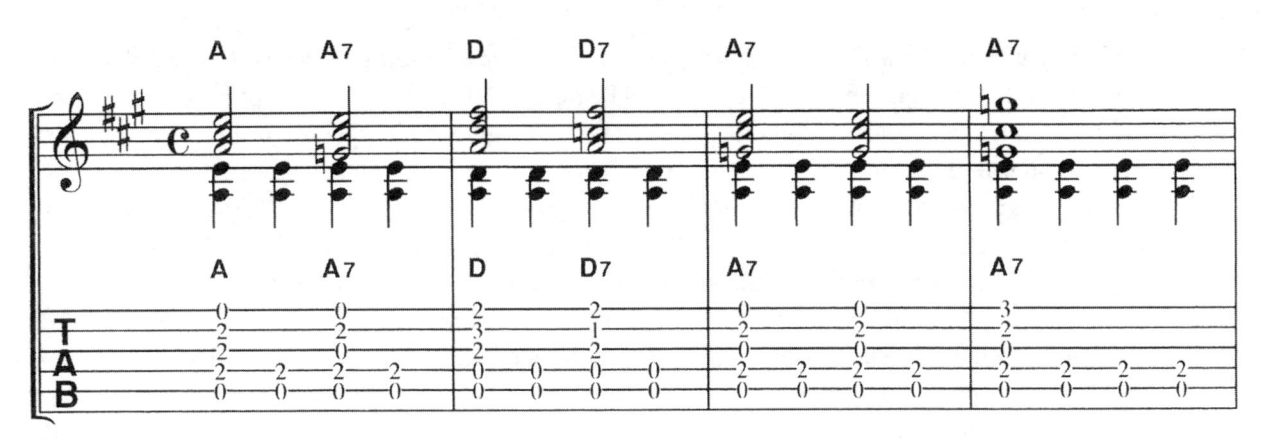

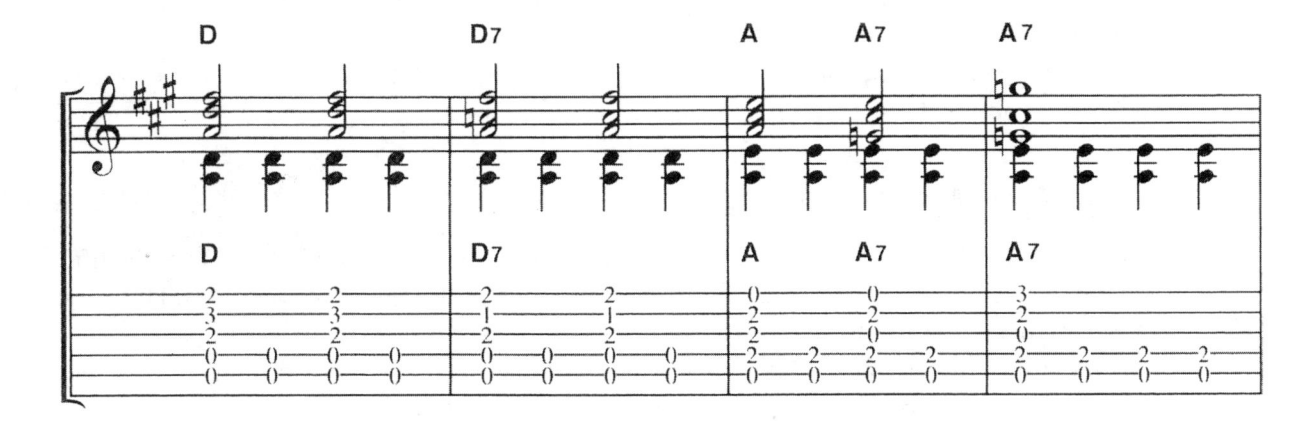

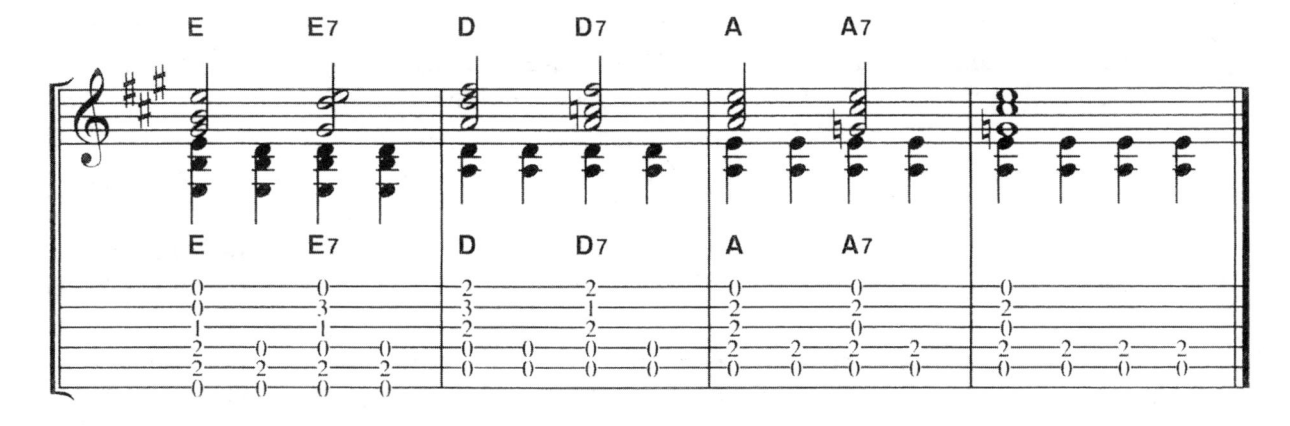

FURTHER WORK 1. You can learn a new chord or a new song or a new lick overnight, but cultivating a touch takes weeks, months, or years. Gradually work towards developing your touch by listening to other guitarists, deciding what you like, getting their sound into your head, and then gradually figuring out what you need to get your body to do to get that sound. Developing a touch requires such delicate nuances of gesture that, in my experience, telling or being told how to do it is of limited use. Best is to find the sound you love in someone's playing and internalizing it until you can absolutely hear it—and also hear, perhaps, that you're not getting it. Pursuing that sound will gradually lead your hands to get it. But if you can't hear what you're after, you won't be able to get it at all.

Here's just one example of the challenging amount of work and devotion it takes to do this:

FURTHER WORK 2: LISTENING. Beg, borrow, or buy the *Eric Clapton Unplugged* CD or DVD (Warner). Listen to Eric Clapton's version of Big Bill Broonzy's "Hey Hey Baby." Clapton is paying homage to Broonzy, who in the 1950s was one of the first American bluesmen to tour England and was a great influence on the seminal British blues scene. It's no insult to Clapton to point out that he's playing Broonzy's notes. Then find one of the several CDs with Broonzy himself playing this song—for example, *Trouble in Mind* on Smithsonian/Folkways. Better yet, get the Rhino *Blues Masters* DVD that has footage of Broonzy thumping away on this masterpiece under the title "Guitar Shuffle." You'll hear and see some of the strongest blues guitar playing you'll ever find, and you'll notice that when Broonzy plays his own piece, he's not playing *notes*, he's playing the *guitar*. (For someone else who also plays with an amazingly strong touch, watch the controlled and strangely delicate brutality with which Son House addresses his guitar on the same DVD. These are musicians who are way beyond worrying about what notes they're playing. They have much bigger things to do.)

On the other hand, perhaps the "real" you is a guitarist who plays with a light and precise touch. Only you can figure that out.

Track 11: Moving Around the A7 Shape

Moving your fingers up the fingerboard makes the notes you are playing higher. Play the fifth string open. Now play the note on the first fret. Now move your finger up to the second fret. The note got higher each time. But you knew that, didn't you?

In written music, we name notes in ascending order using the letters A through G, and then we start with another A all over again. That's seven letters, but there are actually 12 frets on the guitar before we get to that next starting point.

In between the notes named by letter are notes that we call *sharps* or *flats*. *Sharp* means "higher than" and *flat* means "lower than." Taken together as a class, sharps and flats are called *accidentals*. In prose, accidentals can simply be spelled out, or indicated by their notational symbols. Sharp is indicated using the symbol ♯ and flat by the symbol ♭. The plain, ordinary note (that is, without an accidental) is called a *natural* and indicated by the sign ♮. Unless there's some compelling need to use the word *natural* to make things clear, it's usually left out. For example, if you just called a note "A," anyone would assume you meant "A natural." On the other hand, if you were rehearsing a score and incorrectly played an A flat, the conductor would tell you, "No, no, play A natural."

Here's how it works. Let's start on the open fourth, or D, string, which of course sounds a D note. The note on the first fret could be called either D sharp or E flat. (This can be referred to as a *sharp/flat pair*.) The second fret note would be an E. Then E goes right to F and B goes right to C. So here's the way the notes get named, fret by fret on the fourth string:

    D (on the open D string)
    D sharp or E flat (first fret)
    E (second fret)
    F (third fret)
    F sharp or G flat (fourth fret)
    G (fifth fret)

G sharp or A flat (sixth fret)
A (seventh fret)
A sharp or B flat (eighth fret)
B (ninth fret)
C (tenth fret)
C sharp or D flat (eleventh fret)
D (twelfth fret)

(You might be wondering how, with seven letters and seven sharp/flat pairs between them, fourteen note names would fit twelve frets. To solve this problem, the people who developed music theory decided that two of the sharp/flat pairs would be eliminated. B goes right to C; there's no B sharp/C flat in between. Similarly, E goes right to F; there's no E sharp/F flat. In the list of note names above, those two pairs are absent.)

We've just played a *chromatic scale*. A chromatic scale consists of the notes on all 12 frets, every letter and every sharp/flat between them. At the twelfth fret the chromatic scale starts all over again. The thirteenth fret would be D sharp/E flat, and so on. This system of starting all over again on the twelfth fret is rooted in physical reality: It's the exact halfway point of the vibrating string. (The next "halfway point" will be at the 24th fret—though only some electric guitars and a few acoustics have that many frets—at which point you'll get to the next sequence of notes beginning with D.) Each series of 12 frets is called an *octave*. When we got to the D note on the twelfth fret, we were starting a new octave.

Now let's try this on the fifth, or A, string. The open string is A. Playing the first fret gives you A sharp or B flat. The second fret is B. The note on the fourth fret (remember the rule!) is C. The fifth fret is C sharp or D flat. And so on.

What works for notes also works for chord shapes. For example, play an A7 chord, using the shape that bars the second fret and covers the highest four strings. You've got four strings fingered. Now move that chord shape one fret up, so you're playing the bar on fret three instead of on two. (Remember to pluck only the four strings you're fingering: the two open lower strings haven't been moved up along with the others and they won't necessarily sound good played along with them.) You've just moved the chord shape up one fret, so it's now an A sharp 7 (or B flat 7) chord. Now play the shape on the fourth fret; that's a B7 chord. Playing it on the fifth fret gives you a C7 chord; and so on.

Now let's use these shapes to play a 12-bar blues.

PREP WORK. Get used to moving around the A7 shape we've just used. Practice it with the bar on the second fret (A7), with the bar on the seventh fret (D7), and with the bar on the ninth fret (E7). Get used to navigating using the fingerboard dots. Remind yourself of the rule that there are seven letters, with a sharp/flat between every letter except that B goes right to C and E goes right to F without an intervening sharp/flat. Play the barred A7 shape on the second fret and then count it up the fingerboard, calling out the chromatic scale fret by fret, to satisfy yourself that, yes, playing that shape with the bar on the seventh fret is indeed a D7 and on the ninth fret is indeed an E7.

Now we're ready to play Track 11. Note that, as usual, we'll be keeping a steady bass note on the open A string during the A7 chord and on the open E string during the E7 chord. However, with the bar chord shape we're using, the open D string is not available during the D7 chord, so we'll just use the open A string during that chord as well.

Track 11. Moving Around the A7 Shape

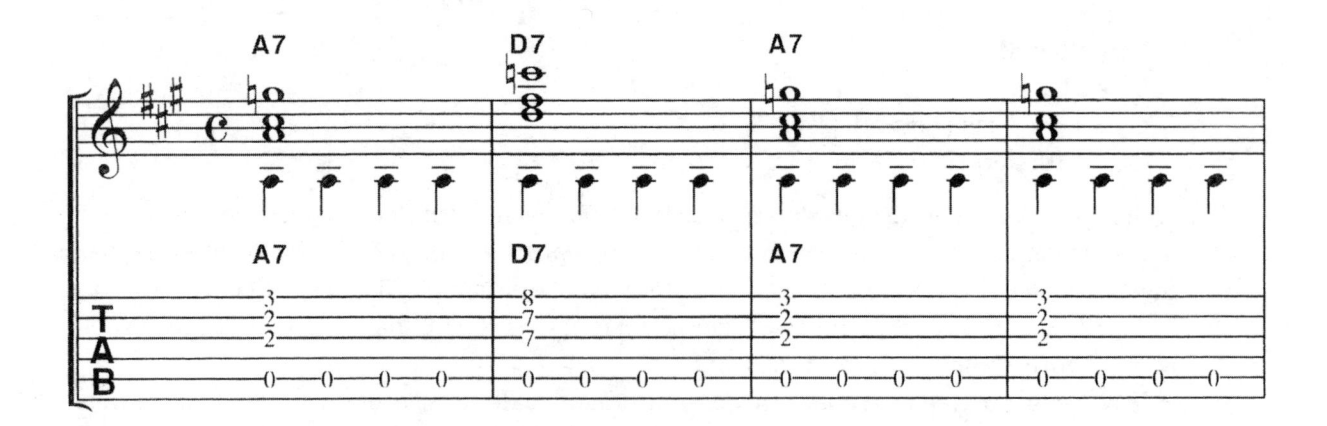

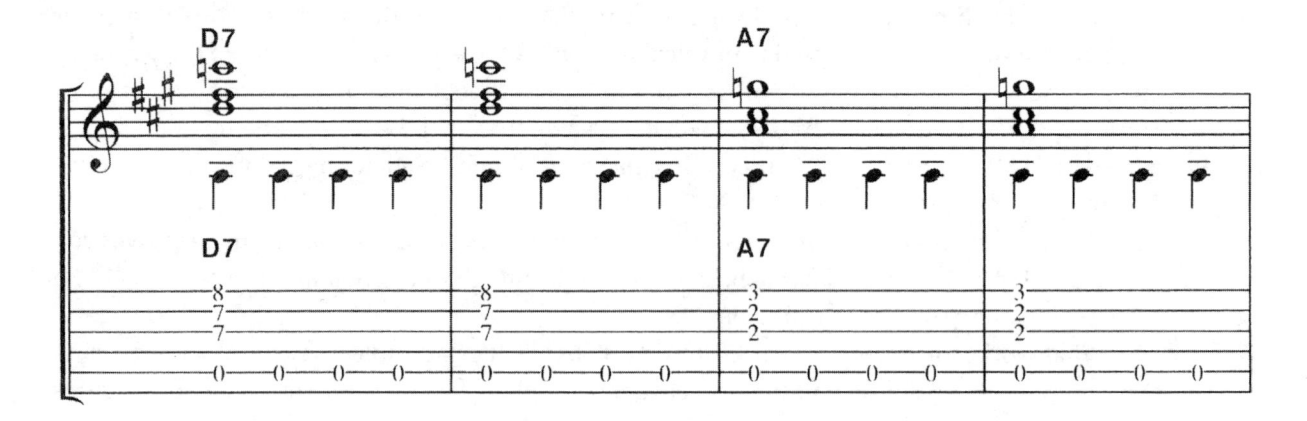

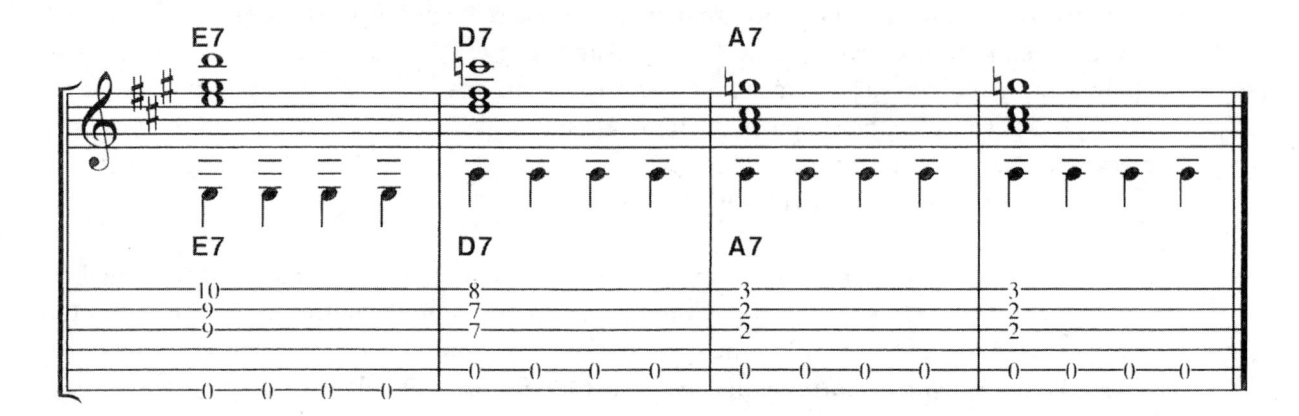

[Notation and tablature for 12-bar blues using A7, D7, and E7 chord shapes]

FURTHER WORK. First get comfortable playing Track 11 accurately and in time. When you can do this, you're ready to apply everything you've learned so far:

- Play the 12-bar blues using the chord shapes from Track 11 but with the rhythm from Track 2 and with any other rhythmic variations you may have come up with.
- Play repeated choruses of Track 11 incorporating the turnaround from Track 3 and the additional turnarounds from Track 5.
- Play the chord shapes in Track 11 using the syncopated rhythm from Track 6.

DISCLAIMER AND DISQUISITION. Truth in packaging requires me to let you know that sometimes, under certain theoretical circumstances, it actually makes sense to use the names B sharp (for the pitch of C), E sharp (for the pitch of F), C flat (for the pitch of B), and F flat (for the pitch of E). So you will occasionally run into these names—though possibly not during your present lifetime.

In addition, you may be wondering why the same pitch should be called, say, either F sharp or G flat. The reasons (so complicated that I don't want to explain them here) can functionally be boiled down to the following: Choosing between using sharps or flats can help make chords and melodies easier to understand. In written music, it also reduces the total number of accidentals that have to be used on the page—sometimes significantly so. This in turn reduces the amount of ink on the page and makes the notes easier to read, the page cleaner to look at, and the sound of the music easier to internalize. It can make a big difference for people who spend their lives dealing with complex written music. For the rest of us, who may just need to yell at the bass player who's playing a wrong note, it doesn't matter that much whether we call it an F sharp or a G flat.

Track 12: Moving Around the D7 Shape

In this track, we'll move around a simple D7 shape in much the same way we moved around the A7 shape in Track 11.

PREP WORK. Let's review the fret counting first. Just as you did in the prep work for Track 11, start with your basic chord, the D7 shape, and count it chromatically up the fingerboard fret by fret. Satisfy yourself that the D7 shape on the eighth fret is indeed an A7 and that the D7 shape on the third fret is indeed an E7. Once again, get used to the feel of where the A7, D7, and E7 are located and how to spot them using both your sense of feel and the fret dots.

Now we're ready to play.

Track 12. Moving Around the D7 Shape

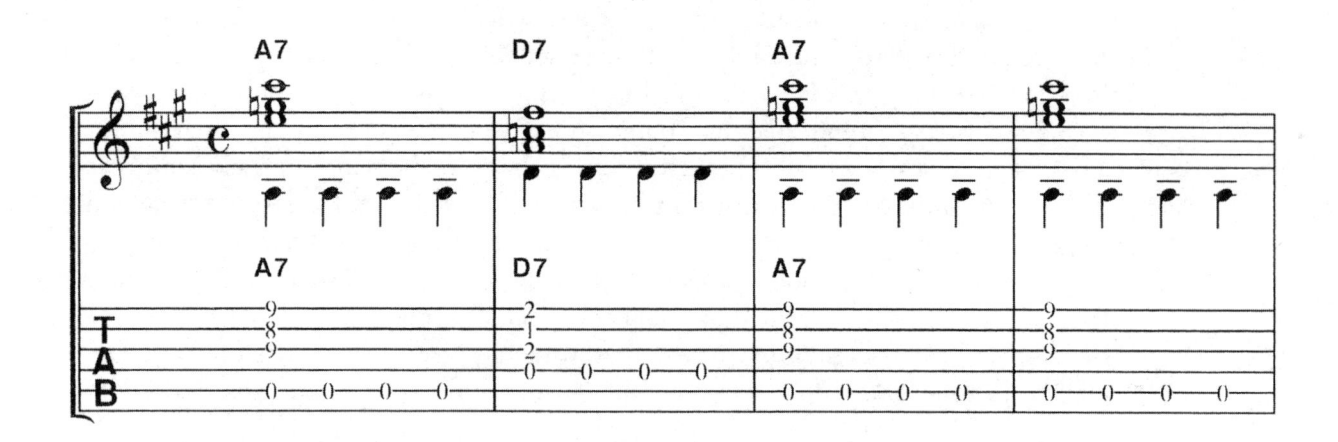

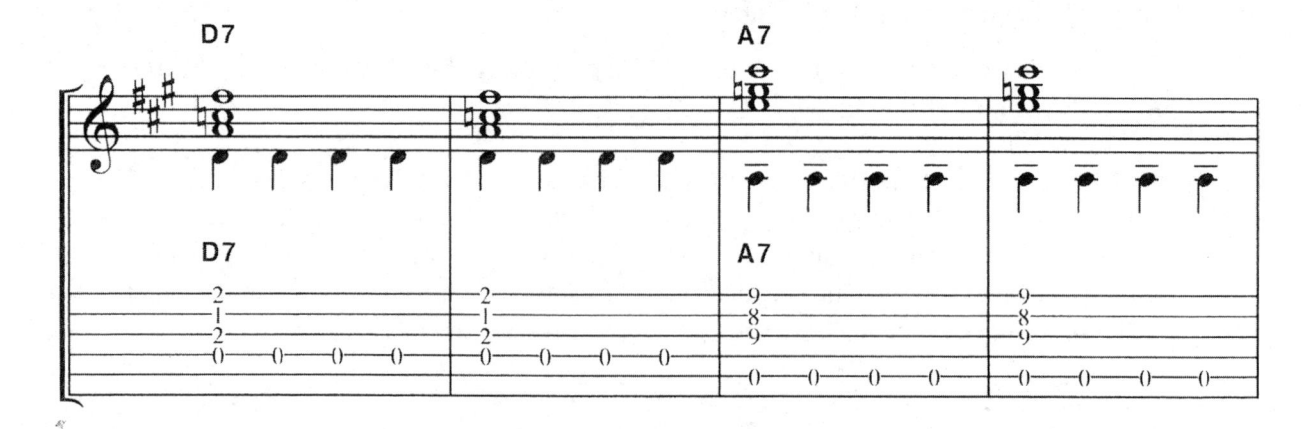

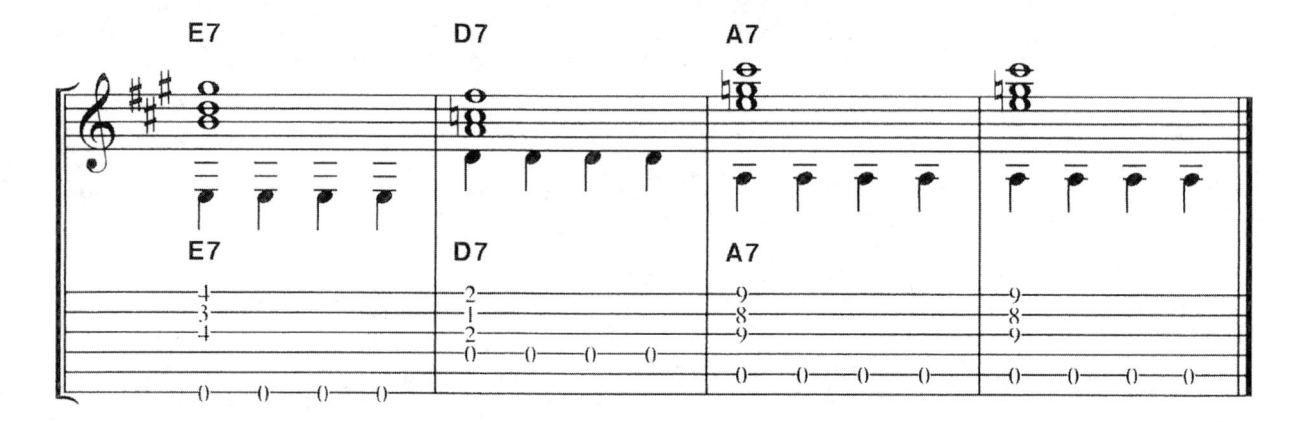

FURTHER WORK. Once you get used to playing the new set of chords, apply the same techniques as you did in the "Further Work" for Track 11.

Tracks 13–14: More Rhythms

The art of playing country blues guitar with a steady bass involves developing the ability to play a variety of different rhythms on the high strings while making sure that you really keep that steady bass note steady. This and the following tracks are exercises in eight such rhythms.

Track 13 is a *syncopated* rhythm. The term *syncopation* refers to accents that are placed off the standard foot-tap in order to give the music some extra bounce, thrust, and drive. In the case of this example, it's a strumming pattern that accents the *upbeats*.

But what's an upbeat? The upbeat is simple enough to understand once you feel it. Just tap your foot, and watch it, and count the beats as it hits the floor. Those are the *downbeats*. The upbeat is the part of the beat where your foot is at its highest. In music, it's common to count the downbeats with numbers: "One, two, three, four, one, two, three, four," and so on. To indicate the upbeat, we say "and," as in "one and two and three and four and one," etc. Each "and" is the half of the beat in between the downbeats. Starting on the upbeat, as this track does, gives the music a unique propulsive thrust.

Track 13. Rhythm 1 (track 14 on CD has this rhythm with 12-bar blues)

Once you master this rhythm as written, on the A7 chord, try it on other chords. Then try going back and forth between two chords. Notice how you'll instinctively feel the chord change coming on the upstroke. You can hear this in Track 14. If you're having trouble with this, skip ahead to Rhythm 8 (Track 27).

Continue to experiment with different chord changes. I think you'll find it especially pleasing (and bluesy sounding) to practice going back and forth from I7 to IV7 in various keys, four or eight beats (thumb notes) on each chord. That would mean:

Key of A: A7 to D7
Key of C: C7 to D7
Key of D: D7 to G7
Key of E: E7 to A7
Key of G: G7 to C7

FURTHER WORK FOR TRACKS 8–24. Experiment with these rhythms on various chord changes and in various keys.

Once you've gotten used to keeping the beat steady through chord changes, apply this rhythm to the entire 12-bar blues. As a challenge, I'm asking you to try this on your own right now. Also apply this rhythm to the blues using the chord shapes from Track 11 and Track 12, and continue to apply the seven rhythms in the next seven tracks in this way.

Tracks 15–16: Rhythm 2

Rhythm 2 is another syncopated rhythm. It differs only subtly from Rhythm 1. In Rhythm 1, the finger strokes for the high notes come out just ahead of the thumb strokes. In Rhythm 2, the first stroke for the high notes comes out ahead of the thumb stroke just as in Rhythm 1, but the second finger stroke is made with a pinching gesture right along with the thumb stroke. It might be easier to learn from listening to the example than by following the verbal explanation.

TRACK 15. RHYTHM 2 (TRACK 16 ON CD HAS THIS RHYTHM WITH 12-BAR BLUES)

Try playing this rhythm over various chord changes, as you did with Rhythm 1. Play around with it, get used to it, and then apply it to the 12-bar blues. Also try adapting it to the chord shapes from Track 11 and Track 12. Also continue to use the following rhythms with the 12-bar blues form, and also continue to experiment with the Track 11 and Track 12 chord shapes.

Tracks 17–18: Rhythm 3

Sometimes it can help get a rhythm in your head to say words along with it. Try saying "Goin' a-WAY..." with this one and with the complete 12-bar version in Track 18 on the CD. (But say "goin" as one syllable.)

TRACK 17. RHYTHM 3 (TRACK 18 ON CD HAS THIS RHYTHM WITH 12-BAR BLUES)

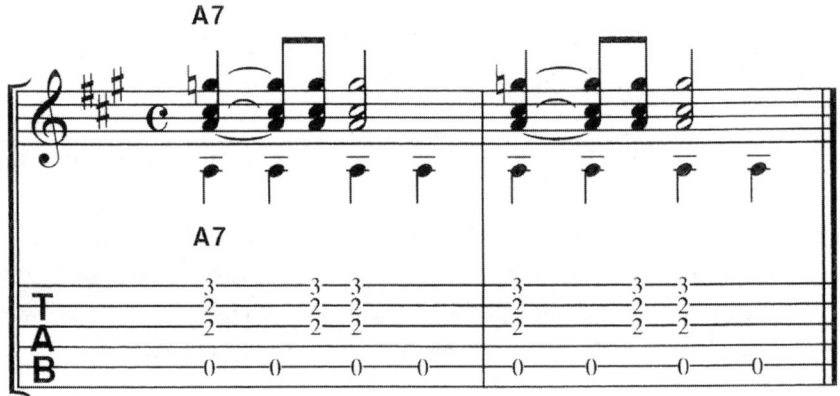

Tracks 19–20: Rhythm 4

This rhythm starts off with the chords on the beat, but subsequent chords come between the thumb notes. On the CD, Track 20 presents the complete 12-bar version.

TRACK 19. RHYTHM 4 (TRACK 20 ON CD HAS THIS RHYTHM WITH 12-BAR BLUES)

Tracks 21–22: Rhythm 5

Try using the words "GOin' a-WAY to STAY now" for this rhythm as it appears in Tracks 21 and on the CD in Track 22. (This wording might be a little deceptive, because there's no syllable that expresses the empty thumb stoke at the end of the pattern. Maybe it's better to say: "GOin' a-WAY to STAY now thump,"

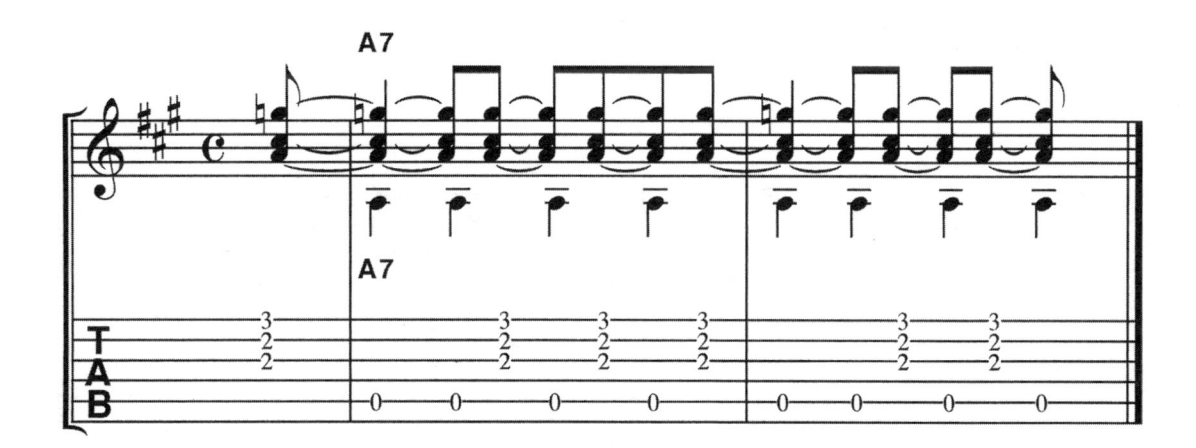

TRACK 21. RHYTHM 5 (TRACK 22 ON CD HAS THIS RHYTHM WITH 12-BAR BLUES)

Tracks 23–24: Rhythm 6

Rhythm 6 is nice and relaxed, good at slow tempos; try playing it at a fast tempo and see whether you agree with me that it's better slow. Some rhythms work better at fast tempos; others slow. The 12-bar version is played on CD Track 24.

TRACK 23. RHYTHM 6 (TRACK 24 ON CD HAS THIS RHYTHM WITH 12-BAR BLUES)

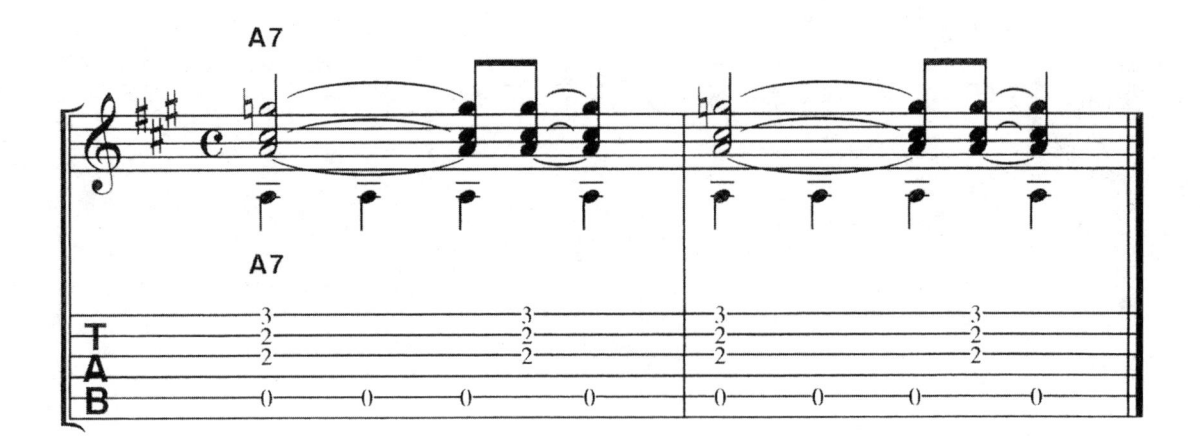

Tracks 25–26: Rhythm 7

This rhythm has almost a marching feel. Truth be told, it's kind of stiff, and I don't like it that much for blues. I offer it mainly as an exercise in control precisely because of its stiffness. If you get tired of the stiffness while playing along with the complete 12-bar version on CD Track 26, then try using the CD just as a metronome and try playing some rhythmic variations of your own along with it.

TRACK 25. RHYTHM 7 (TRACK 26 ON CD HAS THIS RHYTHM WITH 12-BAR BLUES)

Tracks 27–28: Rhythm 8

Let's conclude our rhythm exercises with another syncopated rhythm, accenting the upbeats. Instead of feeling

    ONE and TWO and THREE and FOUR and ONE and TWO...

this rhythm feels like

    AND one AND two AND three AND four AND one AND two...

To get into the flow of the syncopated strum, start on AND. This is another case where the musical example is worth a thousand words, so please listen to Track 27 right now. The thumb plays downward on the bass notes, and in between the thumb beats your index finger (or several fingers; it's up to you) strum or pluck up on the high strings of the A7 chord. Your thumb, moving in a downwards direction, plays the downbeat. Your finger, moving up, plays the upbeat. As you listen to, and play along with, the complete 12-bar version on Track 28, notice how this strum automatically gives you the feeling of the chord change coming ahead of the beat, without having to think too hard—or think at all—about it.

Track 27. Rhythm 8 (track 28 on CD has this rhythm with 12-bar blues)

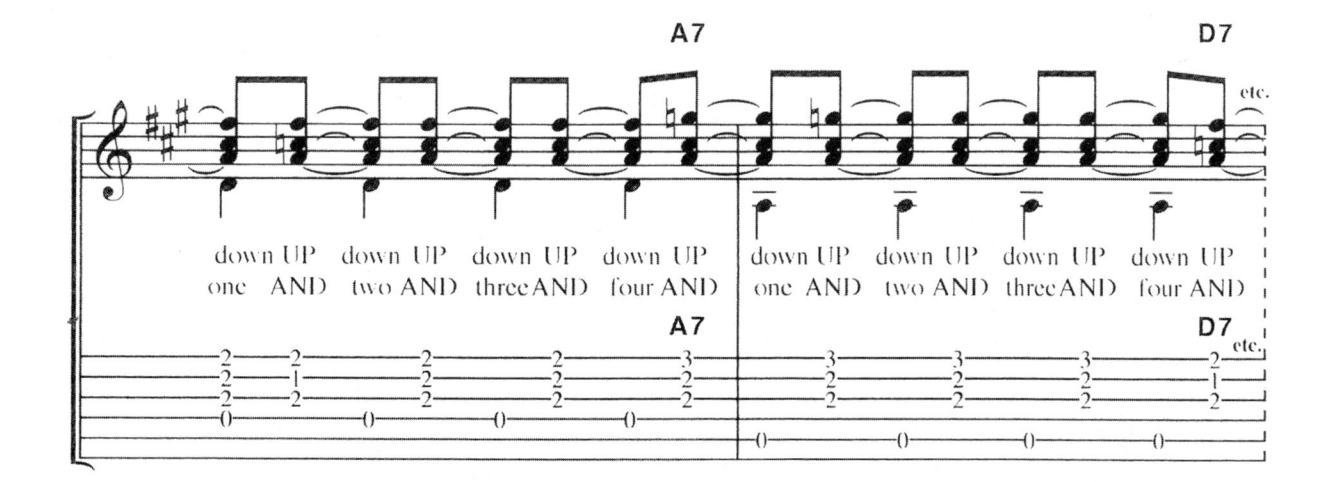

As you listen, you'll notice that the bass note count is really three-and-a-half beats because the upstroke starts on the "and" following the fourth beat. As long as you start this strumming pattern on the upstroke, just the way it's played in the example, it will be easy to get that syncopated flow. If you start playing on a downbeat (with a thumb bass note) and at some later point try to switch around to accenting the upstrokes, you'll find it much more difficult to feel that syncopated flow. Play the example, just going back and forth between the A7 and D7 chords as demonstrated. Listen first; then play along with the example.

Now that you've played it a while, notice that the chord changes occur half a beat *ahead* of the bar line. It's this quality that gives syncopation its forward thrust.

LISTENING. Listen to your blues collection and try to feel which songs, styles, and individual artists take a syncopated approach. Some masters of syncopated up-down strumming are John Lee Hooker, Otis Taylor, and Josh White. (Listen for example, to Hooker's *This is Hip* on Charlie, Taylor's *Below the Fold* on Telarc, and White's *Free and Equal Blues* on Smithsonian/Folkways.) Hooker and Taylor have tremendous drive and complexity. White's gentler, more repetitive sound, on the songs where he plays this way, is like waves cresting on a beach.

FURTHER WORK. You know what you have to do. Take this strumming pattern and apply it to the 12-bar blues (Track 28), and also to the various turnarounds.

PART III

Playing the Blues

In this section we'll learn several fingerstyle country blues guitar solos, each of which is designed to demonstrate a specific technique or cultivate a certain aspect of style. Some of the tracks are related musically to each other, developing concepts or skills in a progressive way and showing how the same basic musical ideas can be expressed in different keys, rhythms, and chord fingerings. For this reason, it makes the best sense to proceed through the following tracks in the order in which they're written.

Track 29: Blues in E: Major and Minor

One of the qualities that give blues music the sound that we instantly recognize as "bluesy" is an interplay between the sound of major and minor. Go rapidly back and forth between an E major and an E minor chord and you'll get the idea. Please get used to the following chord shapes before proceeding to the piece.

Track 29 Chord Chart

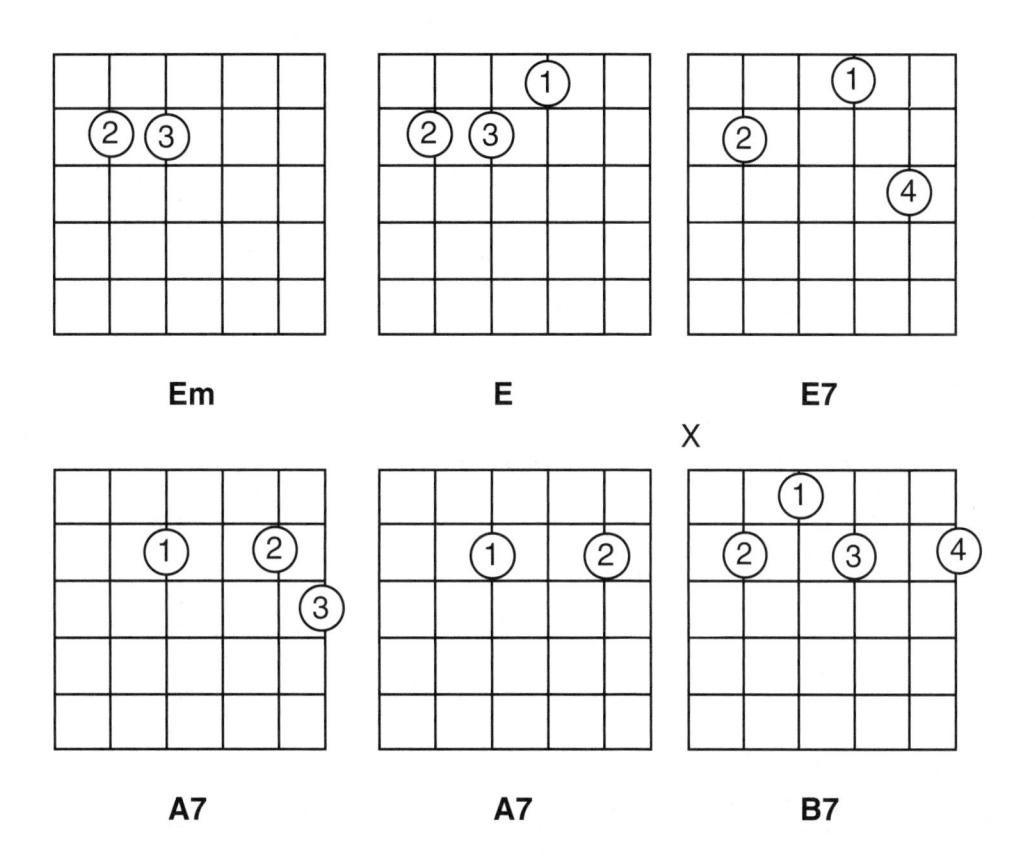

Em   E   E7

A7   A7   B7

47

Track 29 goes back and forth between the sounds of E major and E minor. Notice how the A7 chord shares some of the notes, and much of the sound quality and bluesy soulfulness, of the E minor chord.

Track 29. Major to Minor Blues

FURTHER WORK. As always, continue to rework this piece using the different rhythms you've learned from Tracks 13-28, and incorporating the turnarounds from Track 9. Remember to go on doing this with subsequent tracks as well.

Track 30: Blues in E with Blue Notes and Bending

So far we've learned that seventh chords and minor chords can make the music sound bluesy. Let's add one more, which with an E chord appears on the third string, third fret. Put your pinky down on that note while the rest of your fingers are playing an E or E7 chord and notice how just plain funky it sounds, particularly when it rings with severe dissonance against the open second string.

Track 30 uses all three blue notes played against an E7 chord, emphasizing the bluesy dissonances created by these notes. Finger the E7 chord and then use your pinky for the blue notes, all of which are on the third fret of the top three strings. Notice the sound on the CD of these notes being *bent* slightly upward in pitch by using a slightly wavering upward pressure of the pinky.

Bending notes requires you to develop extra strength in your fingers, and it can especially hard on the naturally weak pinky. If you begin to feel strain or pain in your pinky, stop bending for a while and just play the notes without bending.

Track 30. Blue Notes in E

FURTHER WORK. Try this piece with both clean and brushy styles of picking. Review the text for Track 10 if necessary.

Track 31: Alternating Bass Notes

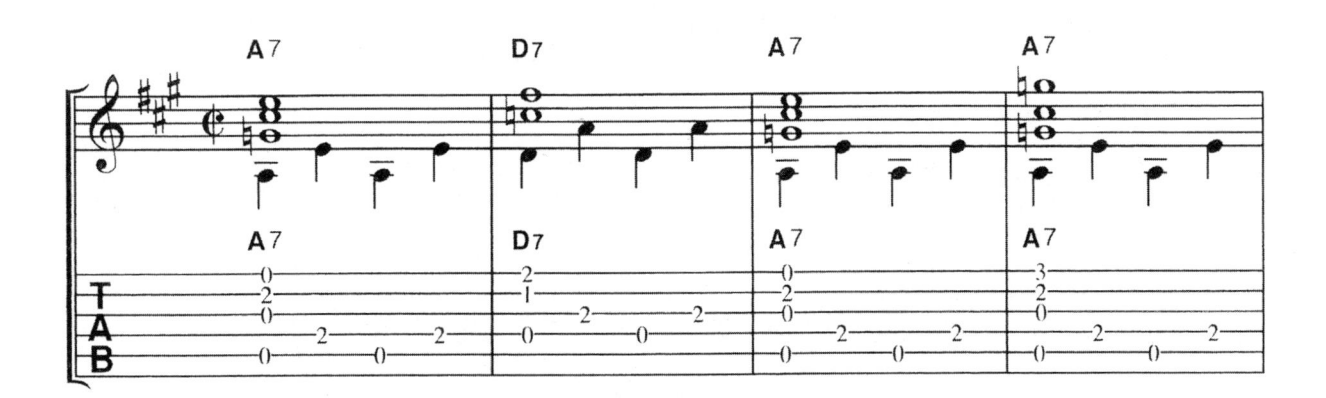

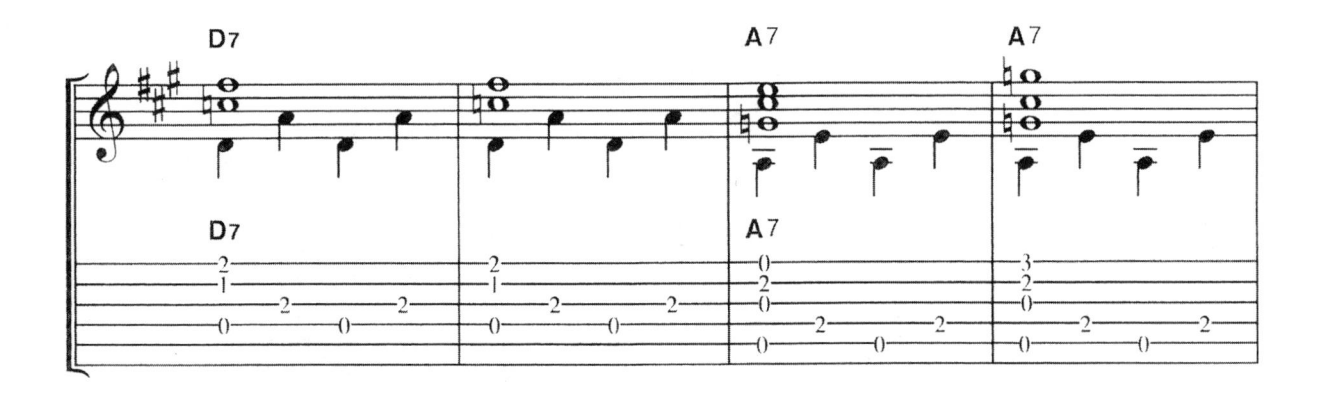

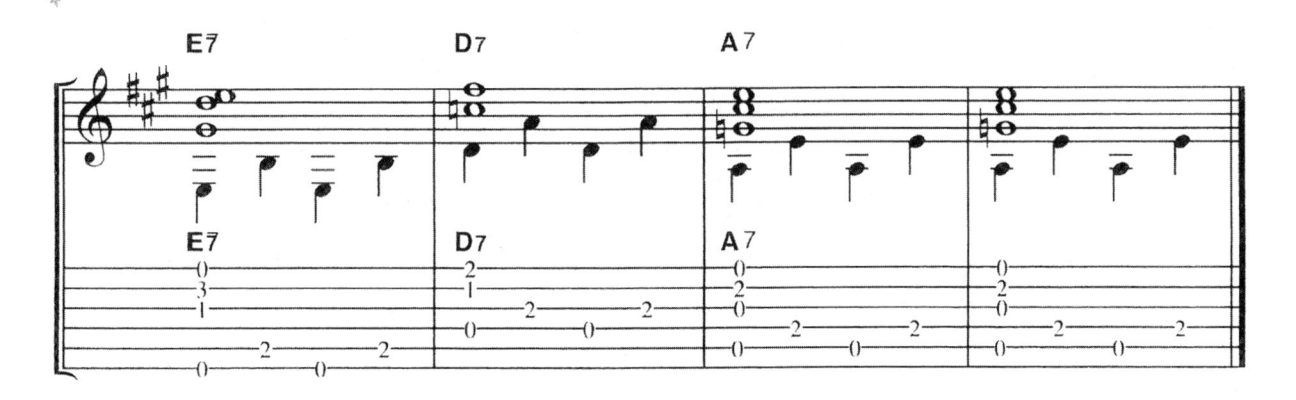

Many country blues styles use the thumb to play alternating bass notes rather than a steady single-note bass. Among the great folk stylists of the early generation, Mance Lipscomb was a guitarist remarkable for the steadiness of his repeated bass notes, while the verve of John Hurt's alternating basses was nothing short of delightful and the odd rhythms of Blind Blake's thumb nothing short of amazing. Here's the basic rhythm of Track 1, redone with alternating bass notes.

TRACK 31. ALTERNATING BASS NOTES

FURTHER WORK. Experiment with alternating basses with the various rhythms you've learned in Part Two. This is easy to say, but hard to do, so don't be deterred if you really have to work at this, even to the point of testing your willpower. Also try working out alternating bass patterns that sound good to you with various chord shapes in other keys.

Sometimes you'll be faced with choices. For example, on a basic G chord shape, you already know that your usual bass note is on the sixth string. But you'll notice that both the fifth and fourth strings are available to you as a possible alternating string. Which one will you choose? Experiment with both, then decide how you want to handle it. John Hurt decided. Bonnie Raitt decided. Paul Simon decided. Bob Dylan decided. I decided. So you decide, too. Just remember: this—like so much of the "further work" I've suggested—is a line of experimentation that you could be returning to for weeks, months, even years.

Track 32: Blues in G

Now that your pinky is nice and strong from playing the preceding track, let's continue to give it a workout by moving it in a similar way against the shapes of G, G7, and C chords. We'll be using an alternating bass in the thumb part, just as in Track 31.

PREP WORK. Get used to the following chord shapes before working on the piece.

Track 32 Chord Chart

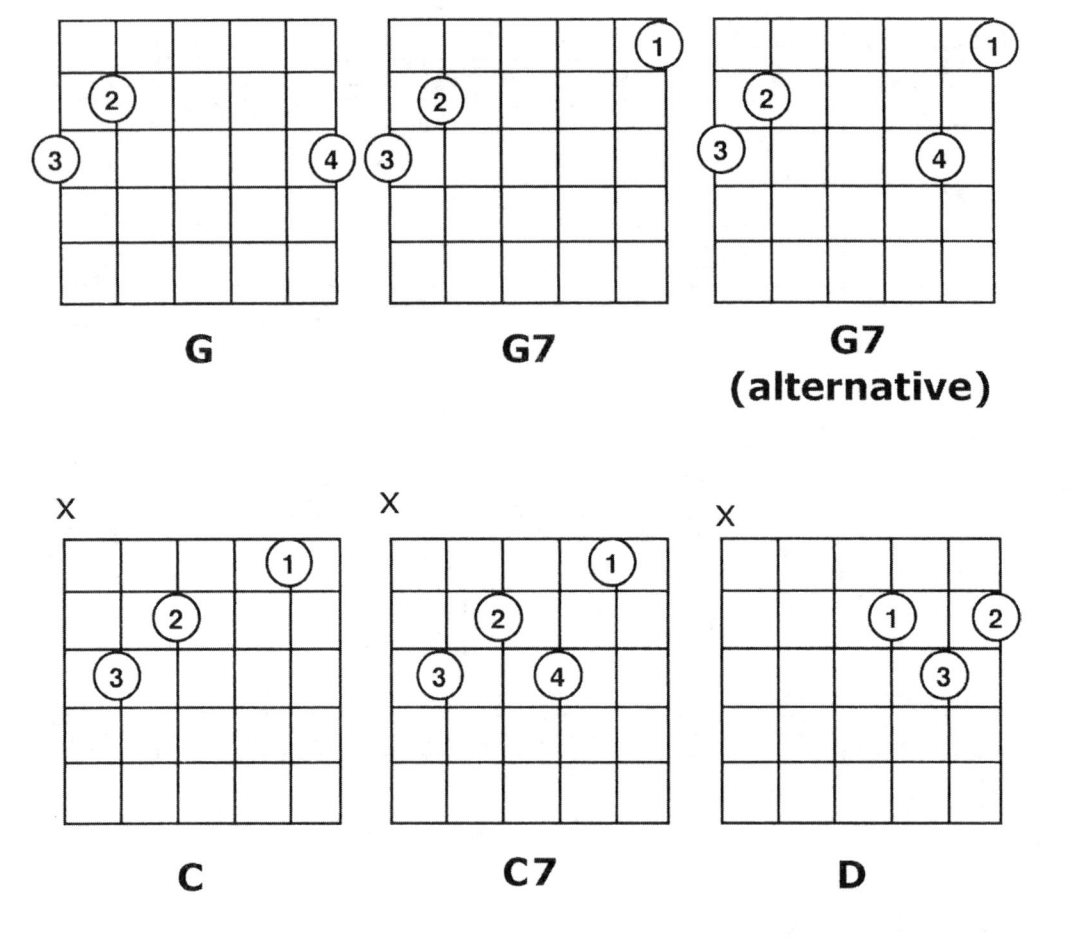

G

G7

G7 (alternative)

C

C7

D

Try experiments on these chord shapes with some of the rhythms you already know, including the alternating bass rhythm from Track 31, before turning to the music from Track 32. I'd like you to do this so that you can experiment without being influenced by my example. Once you've had a little fun with this, proceed with the example.

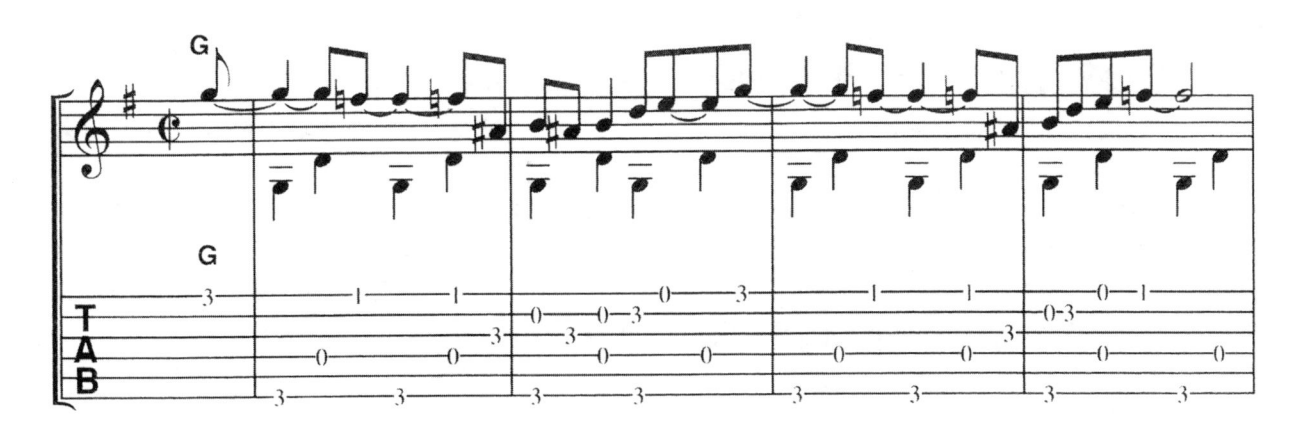

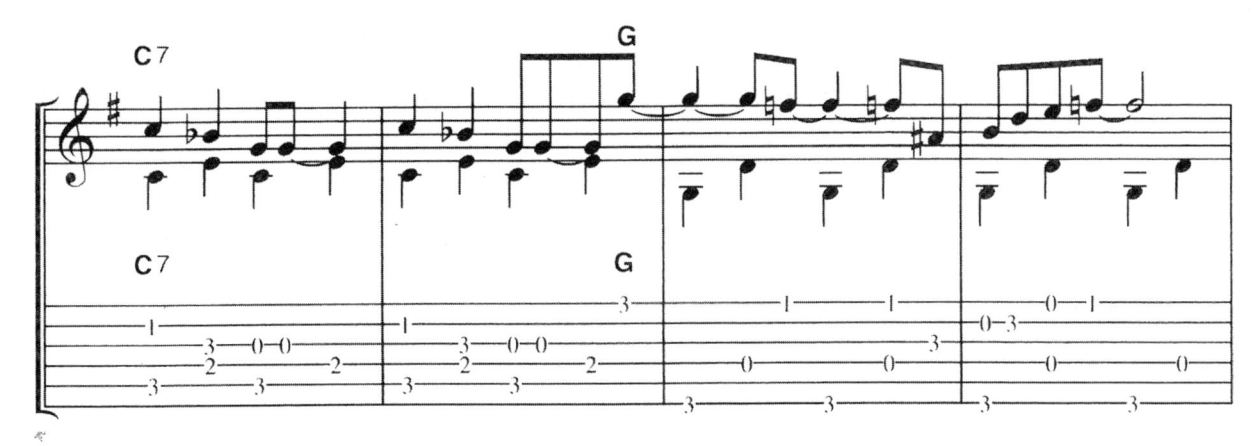

TRACK 32. BLUES IN G WITH ALTERNATING BASS

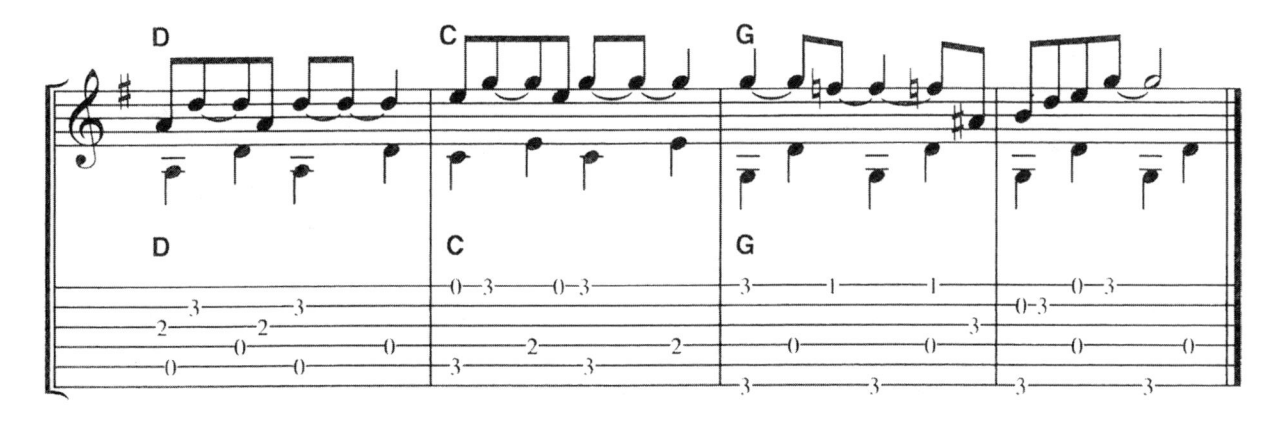

Track 33: Blues in G with Thumping Alternating Bass

Track 32 was played cleanly. Now listen to Track 33. It consists of the bass notes from Track 32, but played this time with broad, brushy thumps of the thumb. This version is followed, after a turn-around, by a version of Track 32, but with the bass in the same broad manner. The brush strokes take in two, sometimes three, strings at a time, even as they alternate from string to string. Try practicing the sound of these bass notes by themselves, as in the first half of the track. Then work on the entire piece.

Track 34: Blues in G with Steady Bass

Track 34 consists of the musical ideas from Track 32, but played with a steady bass instead of an alternating bass. Listen to the sound of the piece on the CD, and then work it out for yourself with no help from written music. In order to do this, you'll need to be secure about playing Track 32, so go back and work on that if necessary.

Track 35: Blues in E with Moveable Chord Shapes

Let's return to the key of E, this time exploring some of the concepts we developed in Tracks 11 and 12.

PREP WORK. Please review Tracks 11 and 12. Now experiment with the following chord shapes and notice how they relate to, and can be explained by, the concepts developed in those tracks.

Playing the Blues

55

Track 35 Chord Chart

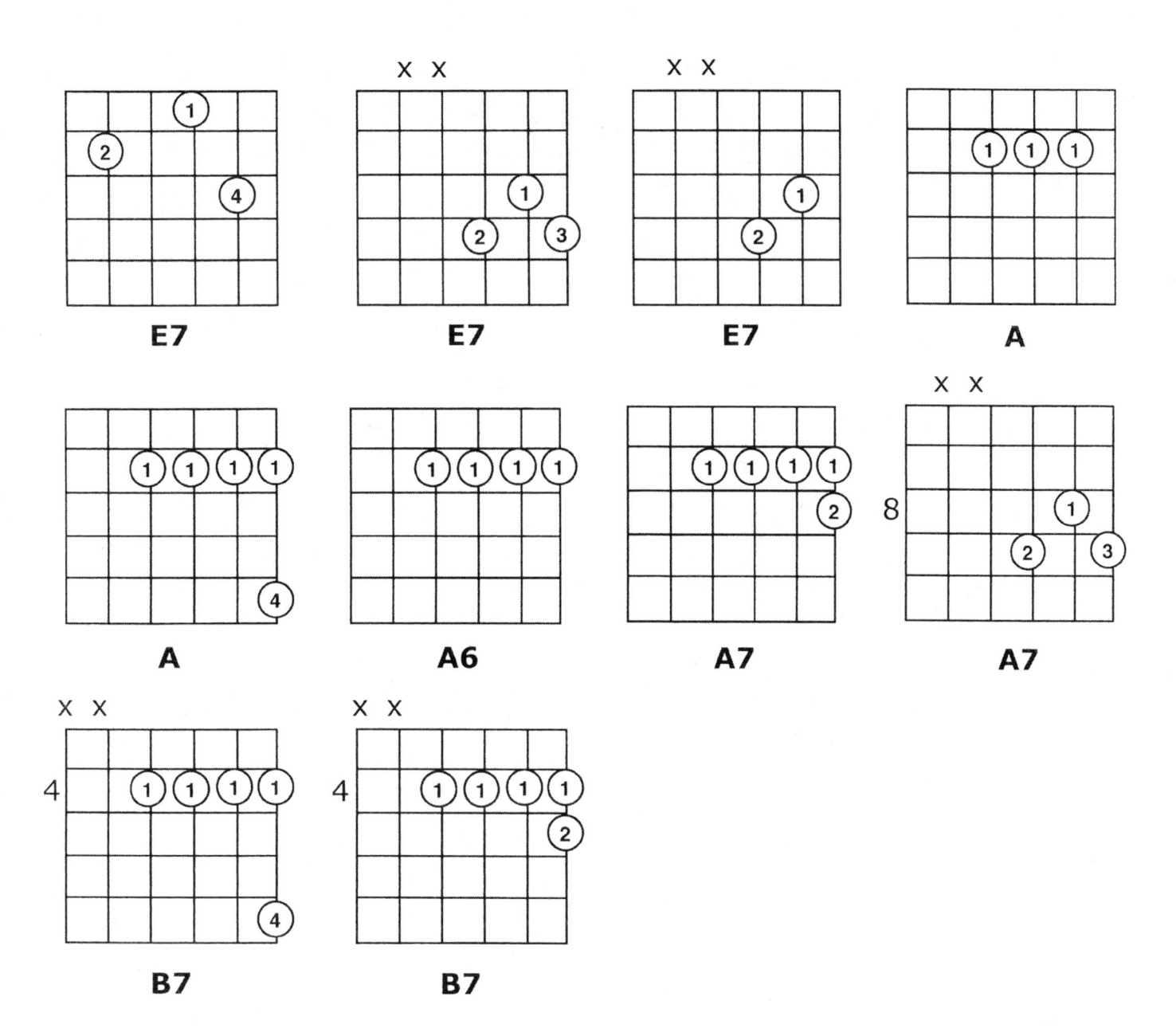

E7   **E7**   **E7**   **A**

A   **A6**   **A7**   **A7**

B7   **B7**

Try playing around with these chord shapes, using different rhythms and touches. Try a steady bass, and then see whether you can find alternating bass patterns that sound good to you. Try doing this one chord at a time. Then go back and forth between any two chords of your choice (but choose chords that sound good together!). Finally, use these shapes in the 12-bar blues progression.

Now we're ready for Track 35.

Track 35. Blues in E with Moveable Chord Shapes

FURTHER WORK. The chord shapes and techniques you've learned in this track are very similar to those used by Big Bill Broonzy and Eric Clapton in "Hey Hey Baby," the piece I recommended you listen to back in Track 10. If you have that piece around on CD or DVD, now would be a good time to pull it out and study it.

This isn't easy, but if you're ambitious you could even try, at this point, to master "Hey Hey Baby" on the basis of what you've learned in Track 35. This is actually the way guitarists learn in the real world, when they're on their own without books and teachers. The more you know, the more you can apply it to what you see and hear other guitarists playing. Notated versions (some incorrect) of "Hey Hey Baby" have been published, but at this point, with help from Track 35, you'd learn more by trying to figure it out on your own.

Track 36: Funky Blues in D with Bending and Vibrato

Now let's turn to the key of D, using chord shapes very similar to those in the preceding track but two frets lower on the fingerboard. In addition, we'll be using a D minor seventh chord that looks like the fingering for a regular D shape, but moved three frets up the fingerboard. Remember that a minor chord and a seventh together make a bluesy sound, so it should be no surprise when you find out that this chord sounds very bluesy indeed. Also notice that this chord is going to get played with the fingers applying some wavering pushing-up motion to the chord shape, "bending" the notes a little and also creating the oscillating effect called *vibrato*.

PREP WORK. Learn the following chord shapes. Go ahead and listen to the CD track now, so you can hear the way vibrato and bending get applied to the D minor 7 chord. To get this effect, press upward with your fingers while keeping your thumb anchored firmly on the back of the fingerboard. If the way you usually play is to support your fretting fingers with the entire heel or palm of your hand on the back of the guitar neck, rather than just the thumb, your fretting hand will probably not be loose enough to make the vibrato.

Track 36 Chord Chart

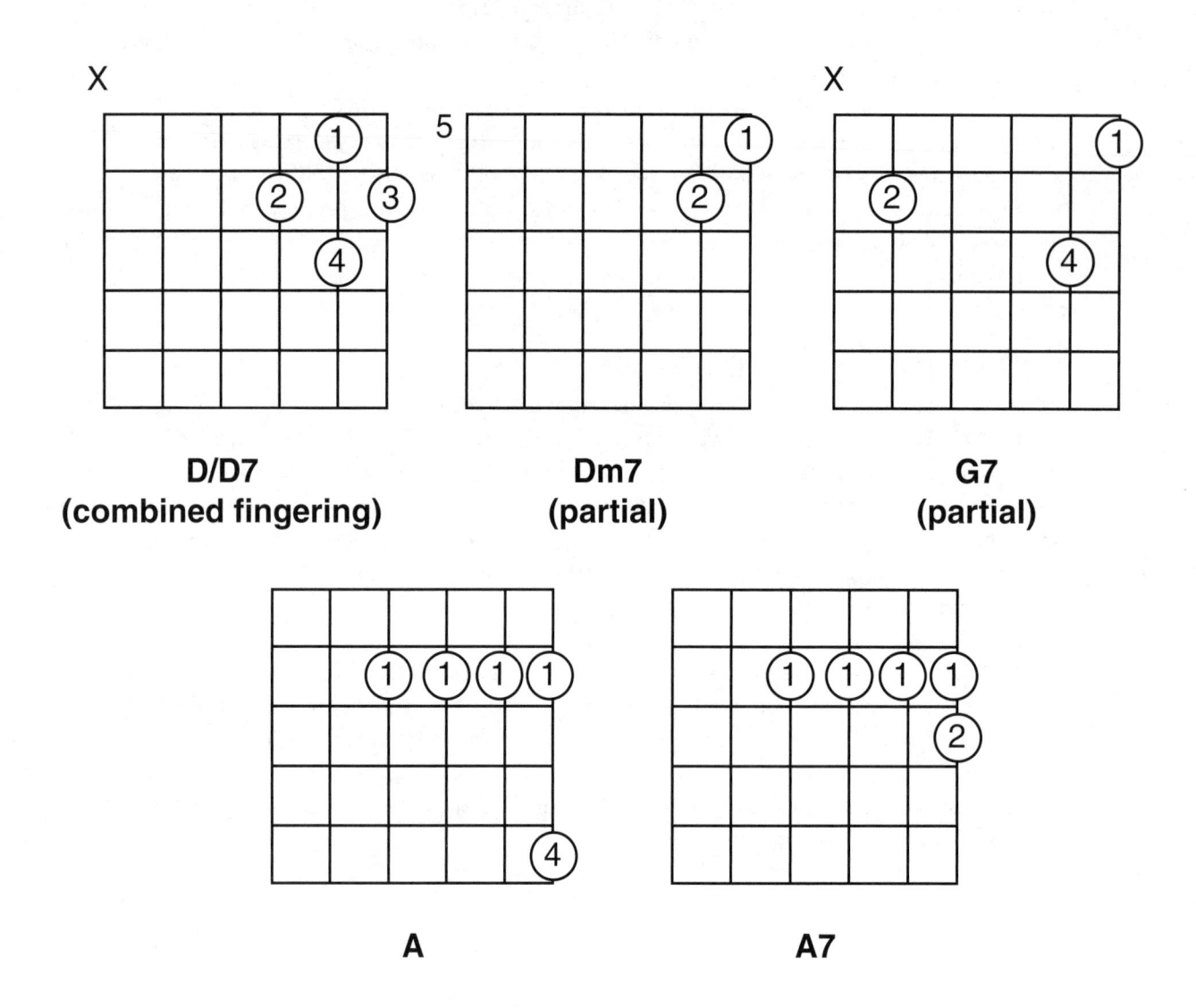

D/D7
(combined fingering)

Dm7
(partial)

G7
(partial)

A

A7

Now let's try the entire blues chorus.

Track 36. Funky Blues in D

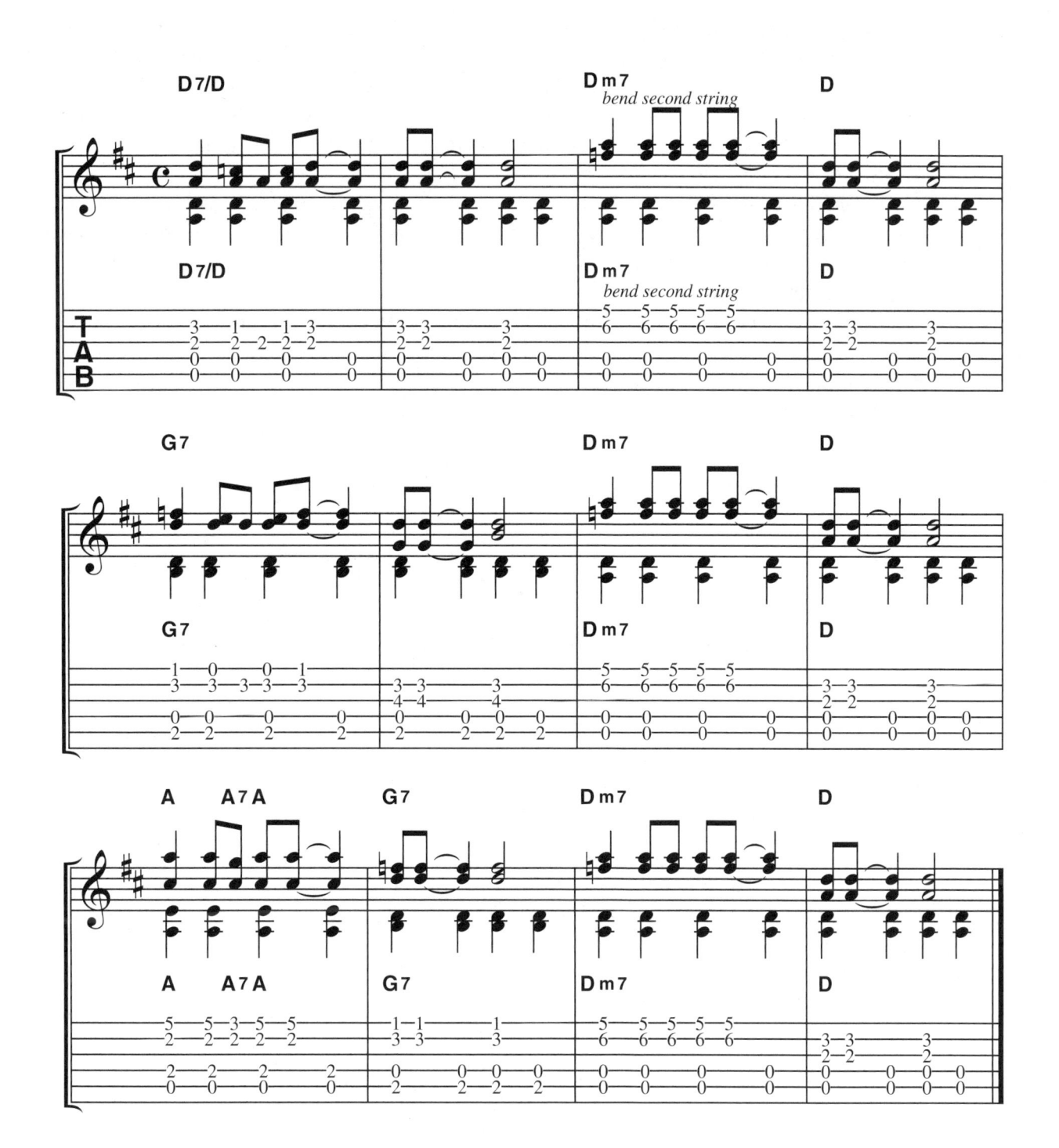

FURTHER WORK. You'll notice that this example is played on the CD in a fairly hard-driving thumping style. Try it with a lighter, cleaner touch. Also try it with alternating bass notes.

Tracks 37–38: Happy Blues in D

By now, you might be noticing the ways in which different keys on the guitar have different sound qualities, different emotional qualities, and different technical possibilities as well. One of the most striking of these is the way the key of D can be made to sound very happy. Among blues guitarists of the first recorded generation, none exploited this capability more than Henry Thomas. Give his Yazoo CD *Texas Worried Blues* a listen; John Hurt, so much of whose music was full of joy, also created many arrangements in D.

This happy blues (Track 37) is an homage to Henry Thomas, though not exactly in his style. Like the other examples on the CD, it's played at a slow tempo so you can catch what's going on and try to play along as you begin to master the piece. But this kind of blues needs to be played at a pretty bouncy clip to really work, so Track 38 presents the same piece played at faster tempo. Notice how the G chord uses the fifth string as the primary bass note. Try using the sixth string instead, and notice the effect of this nuance. To my ear (and, apparently, to the ears of the many other guitarists who use the fifth string like this), the fifth string makes the music seem lighter and brighter.

Playing the Blues

Track 37. Happy Blues in D

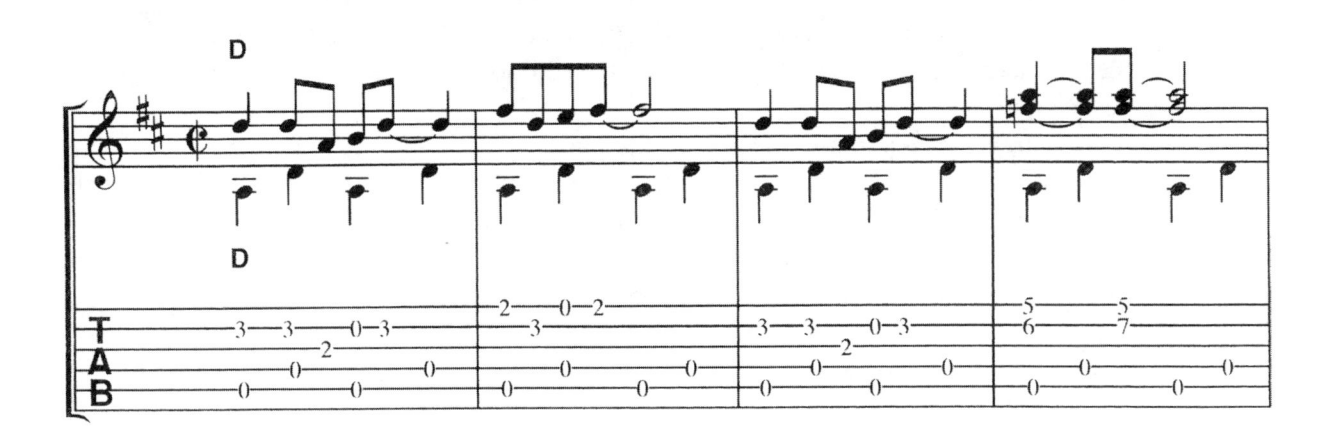

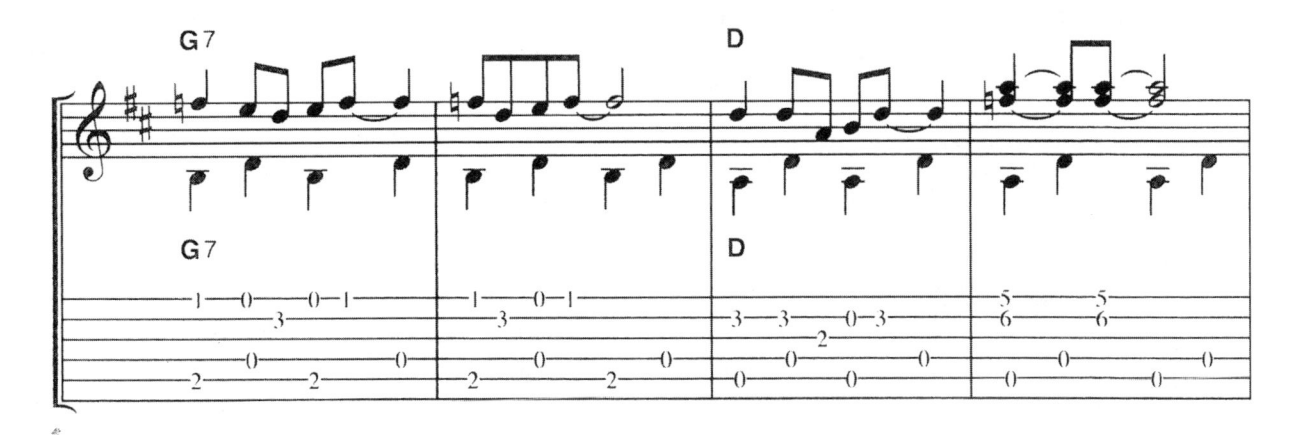

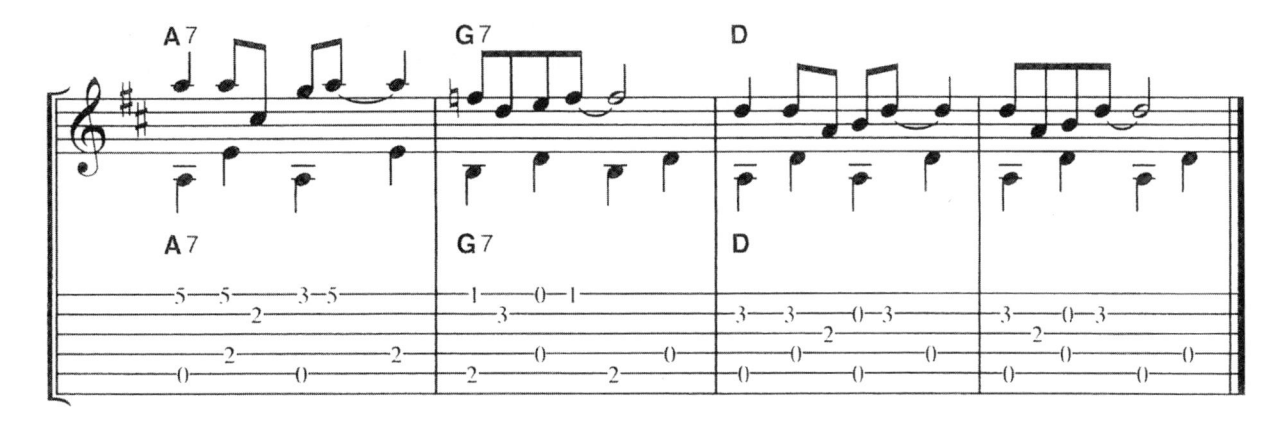

FURTHER WORK. Try to incorporate elements from Track 36—especially the G7 chords and the D minor 7 chords. Slow this piece down, use a steady bass, and try to make it sound less happy. Then go back to Track 36 and try to use elements from Track 37–38 to make Track 36 seem happier. These could include using an alternating bass, playing faster and with more bounce, and using some of the chord shapes and fingerings from Track 37.

Track 39: Working Out A Blues in E

Listen to Track 39 now. What I'm doing here is using some of the ideas and chord shapes from Tracks 36–38, but moving them two frets further up the fingerboard into the key of E. (Remember the chromatic scale: D to D sharp/E flat to E.) In addition, I've changed my thumb notes to fit the new chords.

This is an exercise not only in ear training but in the concept of applying and reworking material you already know in order to learn something new. The track is played very slowly to give you as much help as possible. Even so, it's important to remember in this kind of listening exercise that before even trying to play along, you need to listen to the piece over and over again until you can hear it in your head. Only then are you ready to start.

Track 40: Ragtime Blues in C

Let's conclude with another happy blues, this time in C. For many fingerstyle blues guitarists, C is a light key, the most suitable key for bouncy happy music that reflects ragtime piano. In addition, C is especially conducive for a set of chord changes typical of that piano style. Try playing them with two or four beats on each chord:

A7   D7   G7   C

Blues with a bouncy feeling and these chord changes are often called ragtime blues. Historically, the great ragtime blues guitarists, like Blind Blake and Blind Boy Fuller, came from the eastern seaboard states. They both liked the key of C a lot. (On the other hand, blues players with darker souls, like Lightnin' Hopkins and Robert Johnson, had little use for keys like C and that other happy key, D.) Real piano ragtime is another story completely: historically it precedes blues by several decades, and is structurally closer to nineteenth-century march music than to blues. Here's an example of the way the key of C, with its ample opportunities for alternating basses and ragtime chord changes, gets used for the ragtime blues sound. Notice how in the last four measures, the normal G7–F7–C chord structure is replaced by A7–D7–G7–C.

Playing the Blues

Track 40. Ragtime Blues in C

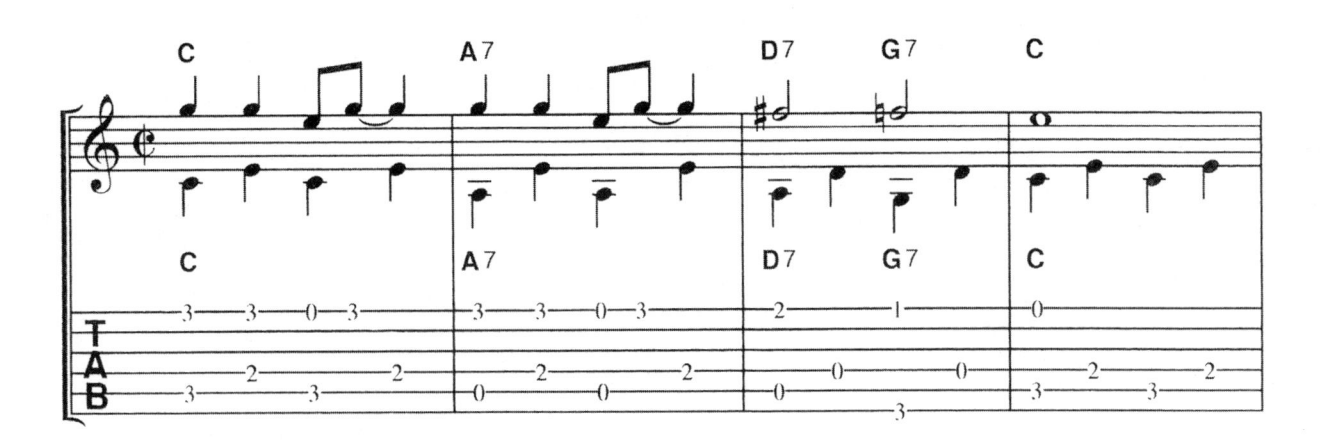

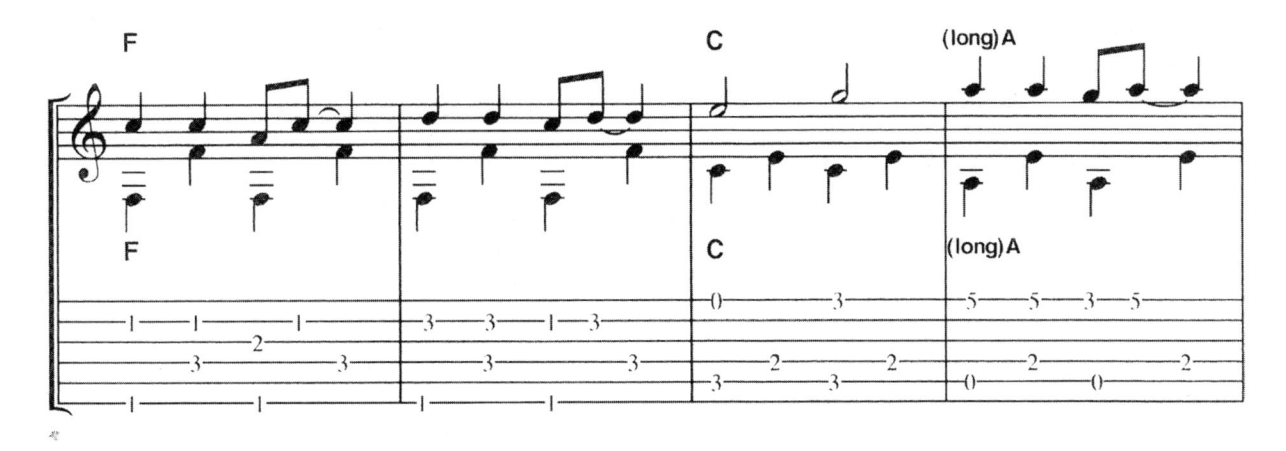

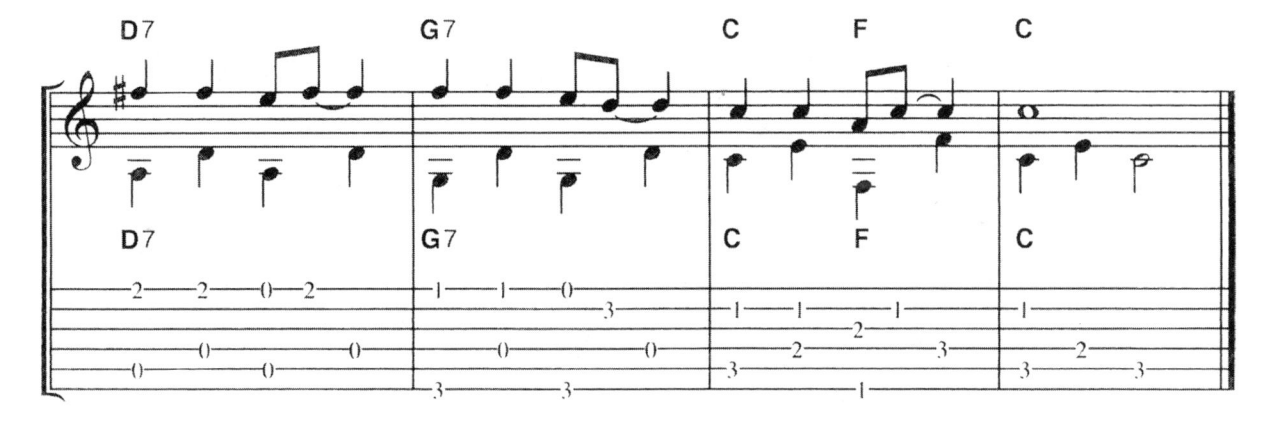

FURTHER WORK. As usual, the CD version is played at a fairly slow tempo in order to make it easier to learn. In real life, a piece like this would be played at a medium to very fast tempo. But as an exercise, try also to play it slowly, with a steady thumpy bass, and to give it as deep and dark a feeling as possible.

Recommended Listening

This is my short list of recommended blues listening from the first recorded generation of blues guitarist-singers. It's very short, but strong. Not all of them play 12-bar blues all the time—or sometimes, at all. Lightnin' Hopkins and Blind Lemon Jefferson are notorious for their excursions out of the strict 12-bar form. John Lee Hooker likes to strum one chord forever—but what a strum and what a chord it is—and then suddenly surprise you with another, but just for a second. Bessie Smith and John Hurt, among others, sing pop and folk songs of their eras, and Reverend Davis sings bluesy hymns and gospel songs. But every guitarist here, in my opinion, is someone that you must hear before you can call yourself knowledgeable about the blues.

Since many of these recordings were made at the dawn of recording science, and were further degraded by rough treatment of the original 78s, don't expect great sound quality. Music lovers can eventually develop the skill of listening through bad sound to great music. (At this point, they also discover that it beats listening through great sound to bad music.) However, be warned that in particular the surviving Blind Lemon Jefferson records have not fared well, and Charlie Patton's are even worse.

In its early days, the world of country blues was mostly a man's world, and certainly the greatest guitarists were men. The most talented women went into another blues world of their own: a world of theatrical blues, performed in tent shows and on vaudeville stages, accompanied by pianists and jazz bands. I've included another must-know, Bessie Smith, to represent this tradition.

Blind Blake: *The Best of* (Wolf)
Reverend Gary Davis and Pink Anderson: *Gospel, Blues and Street Songs* (OBC)
Blind Lemon Jefferson: *The Best of...* (Yazoo)
Blind Willie Johnson: *The Complete* (Sony)
Robert Johnson: *King of the Delta Blues* (Sony)
John Lee Hooker: *This is Hip* (Charly UK)
Lightnin' Hopkins: *The Gold Star Sessions Vol. 2* (Arhoolie)
Mississippi John Hurt: *Avalon Blues (1963)* (Rounder)
Charlie Patton: *Founder of the Delta Blues 1929–34* (Yazoo)
Bessie Smith: *The Collection* (Sony)
Various Artists: *Legends of Country Blues* (JSP)
Muddy Waters: *His Best 1947 to 1955* (Chess)